Behold! A White Horse!

By Stephen Pidgeon

ISBN-13:
978-1453858455

ISBN-10:
1453858458

And I saw when the Lamb opened one of the seals, and I heard, as it were the noise of thunder, one of the four beasts saying, Come and see.

And I saw, and behold a white horse: and he that sat on him had a bow; and a crown was given unto him: and he went forth conquering, and to conquer.

- **Revelation 6:1-2**

PROLOGUE

I considered holding back the specifics of this book from the reading public. My suspicions were first roused in the spring of 2008 as I watched the rise of the gentleman known as Barack Hussein Obama within the ranks of the Democrat Party for its nomination to the office of the Presidency of the United States. Our group undertook our research on this fellow in an ever-continuing state of jaw-dropping revelation. I can remember believing sometime in July of 2008 that we had sufficient enough information to ensure that Obama could never be elected. Yet, with each discovery, the press continued to cover and his numbers continued to rise.

Now, however, my research has astounded me to such a level, that I can no longer merely speculate. It is time to make disclosure about the spirit of this fellow Obama. What you are about to read is intended to elicit a reaction. Some of you may read this as good news; some of you may find these facts totally terrifying; and others may reject it outright as more of that Christian *tin hat* nonsense.

Some have called him a Manchurian Candidate – an unwitting operative for the Communist Party. Others have called him an operative for the New World Order (NWO) to the extent something like that exists.

Behold! A white horse! is an exposé of those scriptures related to what so many my assume is an *Antichrist (*as differentiated from *the* Antichrist*),* and reaches the conclusion that the *white horse Antichrist* is among us even now, in the persona we know as Barack Hussein Obama.

Yes, the title of *Antichrist* has been applied to every significant world leader since Adolf Hitler, people finding a way to extrapolate some derivation of the gamatria of 666 to conclusively prove that the person in question is the so-called *Antichrist*. In most cases, these summaries were true; the person involved was in fact an Antichrist, denying that Christ had come in the flesh.

However, the case of Barack Hussein Obama is an interesting one, well beyond finding a correlation between 666 and the letters of his name. In fact, I would not make the argument that the Greek letters Kai, Psi, and Sigma even mean six hundred, sixty and six. There are so many other arguments, and the true application of Kai, Psi, and Sigma may give even more reason to point the finger at Obama as "the one". As we read here, we will most certainly find that he is "a one", but, notwithstanding Oprah's claim, only time will tell if he is "the one"

The person who will appear just before the return of Christ that many call *the Antichrist* as defined in 1 John and 2 John is also understood as *the beast who rises from the earth, the Assyrian,* and *the False Prophet,* among others. The leader that will rise is better under stood under the identity of the *man of lawlessness*, rather than the *Antichrist*.

For those who have applied 666 to this person or that, such application ignores that the *pseudo-Christ* must satisfy *all* of the prophecies, not just a 666 enumeration.

My argument here is that the *white horse* of Revelation 6 is also an *Antichrist* – a man of lawlessness, a counterfeit Christ. I will gather those prophecies here, and then compare them to the facts concerning our man Barack Hussein Obama as we know them. Time is short and the Kingdom of Heaven draws near. If you come to agree with the conclusion made herein, but have not confessed Jesus Christ as your personal savior, the time is now. Get right with Yeshua, and avoid the rush.

Here is the truth of the gospel so you might know of it.

> Beloved, let us love one another: for love is of God; and every one that loveth is born of God, and knoweth God.
>
> He that loveth not knoweth not God; for God is love.

In this was manifested the love of God toward us, because that God sent his only begotten Son into the world, that we might live through him.

Herein is love, not that we loved God, but that he loved us, and sent his Son to be the propitiation for our sins.

Beloved, if God so loved us, we ought also to love one another.

No man hath seen God at any time. If we love one another, God dwelleth in us, and his love is perfected in us.

Hereby know we that we dwell in him, and he in us, because he hath given us of his Spirit.

And we have seen and do testify that the Father sent the Son to be the Saviour of the world.

Whosoever shall confess that Jesus is the Son of God, God dwelleth in him, and he in God.

1 John: 4-7-15

TABLE OF CONTENTS

PART ONE:

THE TIMING OF THE ARRIVAL OF

THE MAN OF LAWLESSNESS

PART TWO:

THE IDENTITY OF THE MAN OF LAWLESSNESS

PART THREE:

THE ACTIONS OF THE MAN OF LAWLESSNESS

PART ONE:

THE TIMING OF THE ARRIVAL OF THE MAN OF
LAWLESSNESS

CHAPTER ONE

The Decrees to Rebuild the Temple
and Jerusalem

Cyrus the Great

We begin our quest to discover the nature and times of the man of lawlessness by first journeying back to the days of Cyrus the Great. Even before Cyrus the Great, the prophet Isaiah, during the later part of the 8th century B.C., sometime before 742 B.C and continuing into the reign of Hezekiah in 715 B.C. had this to say about Cyrus:

> The vision of Isaiah the son of Amoz, which he saw concerning Judah and Jerusalem in the days of Uzziah [783 BC-742 BC], Jotham, Ahaz, and Hezekiah [715-687 BC], kings of Judah. Isaiah 1:1.

> Thus saith the LORD, thy redeemer, and he that formed thee

from the womb, I am the LORD that maketh all things; that stretcheth forth the heavens alone; that spreadeth abroad the earth by myself;

That frustrateth the tokens of the liars, and maketh diviners mad; that turneth wise men backward, and maketh their knowledge foolish;

That confirmeth the word of his servant, and performeth the counsel of his messengers; that saith to Jerusalem, **Thou shalt be inhabited; and to the cities of Judah, Ye shall be built, and I will raise up the decayed places thereof**:

That saith to the deep, Be dry, and I will dry up thy rivers:

That saith of Cyrus, He is my shepherd, and shall perform all my pleasure: even saying to Jerusalem, Thou shalt be built; and to the temple, Thy foundation shall be laid.   Isaiah 44:24-28.

Isaiah goes on to set out a special anointing on Cyrus, as follows:

Thus saith the LORD to his anointed, **to Cyrus, whose right hand I have holden, to subdue nations before him; and I will loose the loins of kings, to open before him the two leaved gates; and the gates shall not be shut;**

I will go before thee, and make the crooked places straight: I will break in pieces the gates of brass, and cut in sunder the bars of iron:

And I will give thee the treasures of darkness, and hidden riches of secret places, that thou mayest know that I, the LORD, which call thee by thy name, am the God of Israel.

For Jacob my servant's sake, and Israel mine elect, **I have even called thee by thy name: I have**

surnamed thee, though thou hast not known me.

I am the LORD, and there is none else, there is no God beside me: I girded thee, though thou hast not known me:

That they may know from the rising of the sun, and from the west, that there is none beside me. I am the LORD, and there is none else.

I form the light, and create darkness: I make peace, and create evil: I the LORD do all these things.

Drop down, ye heavens, from above, and let the skies pour down righteousness: let the earth open, and let them bring forth salvation, and let righteousness spring up together; I the LORD have created it.

Woe unto him that striveth with his Maker! Let the potsherd strive with the potsherds of the earth. Shall the clay say to him that fashioneth it, What makest thou? or thy work, He hath no hands?

Woe unto him that saith unto his father, What begettest thou? or to the woman, What hast thou brought forth?

Thus saith the LORD, the Holy One of Israel, and his Maker, Ask me of things to come concerning my sons, and concerning the work of my hands command ye me.

I have made the earth, and created man upon it: I, even my hands, have stretched out the heavens, and all their host have I commanded.

I have raised him up in righteousness, and I will direct all his ways: he shall build my city, and he shall let go my captives, not for price nor reward, saith the LORD of hosts. Isaiah 45:1-13.

So, there is the prophecy, set forth sometime during the reign of Hezekiah, sometime before 687 BC.

Cyrus the Great (576 – 529 BC) arrived on the scene over 100 years later. He rose to unify the Persian and Median empires as part of the Achaemenid dynasty. In his 29 year reign, he conquered the Median empire, the Lydian empire and the Chaldean empire (three "ribs" if you will), creating the largest empire in the world at that time. He died fighting the Scythians in Syr Darya, an area around the Aral Sea in modern day Kazakhstan.

Cyrus the Great conquered Babylon during the reign of the son of Nebuchadnezzar whose name was Nabonidus. Nabonidus ruled with a person described as either his son or his brother, the heir of Nebuchadnezzar named Belshazzar in the year 539 B.C., specifically, on October 13, 539 B.C. The story of this victory is quite incredible, as the great city was taken without a battle.

According to the historian Herodotus, Cyrus's armies diverted the Euphrates River into a canal so that the water level dropped to the height of the middle of a man's thigh, which allowed the Persian troops to march directly through the river bed into the city and to enter the city at night. Cyrus himself entered the city and confronted Nabonidus, who immediately surrendered.

To gain some understanding of the timing on this, take a look at the book of Daniel.

> Now at the end of the days that the king had said he should bring

them in, then the prince of the eunuchs brought them in before Nebuchadnezzar.

And the king communed with them; and among them all was found none like Daniel, Hananiah, Mishael, and Azariah: therefore stood they before the king.

And in all matters of wisdom and understanding, that the king enquired of them, he found them ten times better than all the magicians and astrologers that were in all his realm.

And Daniel continued even unto the first year of king Cyrus. Daniel 1:18-21.

Daniel was empowered as a counselor to the king of the Babylonian empire even into the first year of Cyrus the Great, or through 539 BC. There are those who believe that Daniel read the prophecy of Isaiah to

Cyrus, and that as a result, Cyrus entered the decree as prophesized in Isaiah 44:28: **That saith of Cyrus, He is my shepherd, and shall perform all my pleasure: even saying to Jerusalem, Thou shalt be built; and to the temple, Thy foundation shall be laid**.

Fortunately, there is an exact record of this decree.

> Now in the first year of Cyrus king of Persia [539 BC], that the word of the LORD by the mouth of Jeremiah might be fulfilled, the LORD stirred up the spirit of Cyrus king of Persia, that he made a proclamation throughout all his kingdom, and put it also in writing, saying,
>
> Thus saith Cyrus king of Persia, The LORD God of heaven hath given me all the kingdoms of the earth; and he hath charged me to build him an house at Jerusalem, which is in Judah.
>
> Who is there among you of all his people? his God be with him, and

let him go up to Jerusalem, which is in Judah, and build the house of the LORD God of Israel, (he is the God,) which is in Jerusalem.

And whosoever remaineth in any place where he sojourneth, let the men of his place help him with silver, and with gold, and with goods, and with beasts, beside the freewill offering for the house of God that is in Jerusalem.

Then rose up the chief of the fathers of Judah and Benjamin, and the priests, and the Levites, with all them whose spirit God had raised, to go up to build the house of the LORD which is in Jerusalem.

And all they that were about them strengthened their hands with vessels of silver, with gold, with goods, and with beasts, and with precious things, beside all that was willingly offered.

Also Cyrus the king brought forth the vessels of the house of the LORD, which Nebuchadnezzar had brought forth out of Jerusalem, and had put them in the house of his gods;

Even those did Cyrus king of Persia bring forth by the hand of Mithredath the treasurer, and numbered them unto Sheshbazzar, the prince of Judah.

And this is the number of them: thirty chargers of gold, a thousand chargers of silver, nine and twenty knives,

Thirty basons of gold, silver basons of a second sort four hundred and ten, and other vessels a thousand.

All the vessels of gold and of silver were five thousand and four hundred. All these did Sheshbazzar bring up with them of the captivity that were brought up from Babylon unto Jerusalem. Ezra 1:1-11.

Xerxes I

This is not the end of the story, however. Although the decree of Cyrus was made in 539 BC, the foundation for the temple was not laid until the following year, or 538 BC.

> Now in the second year of their coming unto the house of God at Jerusalem, in the second month, began Zerubbabel the son of Shealtiel, and Jeshua the son of Jozadak, and the remnant of their brethren the priests and the Levites, and all they that were come out of the captivity unto Jerusalem; and appointed the Levites, from twenty years old and upward, to set forward the work of the house of the LORD.
>
> Then stood Jeshua with his sons and his brethren, Kadmiel and his sons, the sons of Judah, together, to set forward the workmen in the house of God: the sons of Henadad, with

their sons and their brethren the Levites.

And when **the builders laid the foundation of the temple** of the LORD, they set the priests in their apparel with trumpets, and the Levites the sons of Asaph with cymbals, to praise the LORD, after the ordinance of David king of Israel. Ezra 3:8-10

There was opposition to the rebuilding of Jerusalem, however, which began in the first year of the reign of Xerxes I, around 485 BC. Xerxes I, was the son of Darius the Great and Atossa, the daughter of Cyrus the Great. He was also the husband of Esther; consequently, the opposition to the construction fell on deaf ears.

Artaxerxes

Following the death of Xerxes I, a group of Syrians wrote the new king

Artaxerxes and complained anew.

Artaxerxes had obtained the throne in 465 BC only after he had murdered his older brother Darius. When Artaxerxes had determined that sedition was a possibility of the city was rebuilt, he gave the command to make them cease, and work halted until the second year of Darius king of Persia.

Darius II

Xerxes II succeeded his father Artaxerxes only to be assassinated 45 days later by his brother Sogdianus, who in turn was murdered by Darius II. Darius reigned in Persia from 423 BC to 404 BC. Now in the year 422 BC, Haggai made the following prophecy:

> In the second year of Darius the king, in the sixth month, in the first day of the month, came the word of the LORD by Haggai the prophet unto

Zerubbabel the son of Shealtiel, governor of Judah, and to Joshua the son of Josedech, the high priest, saying,

Thus speaketh the LORD of hosts, saying, This people say, The time is not come, the time that the LORD's house should be built.

Then came the word of the LORD by Haggai the prophet, saying,

Is it time for you, O ye, to dwell in your cieled houses, and this house lie waste?

Now therefore thus saith the LORD of hosts; Consider your ways.

Ye have sown much, and bring in little; ye eat, but ye have not enough; ye drink, but ye are not filled with drink; ye clothe you, but there is none warm; and he that earneth wages earneth wages to put it into a bag with holes.

Thus saith the LORD of hosts;
Consider your ways.

Go up to the mountain, and
bring wood, and build the house; and I
will take pleasure in it, and I will be
glorified, saith the LORD.

Ye looked for much, and, lo it
came to little; and when ye brought it
home, I did blow upon it. Why? saith
the LORD of hosts. Because of mine
house that is waste, and ye run every
man unto his own house.

Therefore the heaven over you
is stayed from dew, and the earth is
stayed from her fruit.

And I called for a drought upon
the land, and upon the mountains, and
upon the corn, and upon the new
wine, and upon the oil, and upon that
which the ground bringeth forth, and
upon men, and upon cattle, and upon
all the labour of the hands.

Then Zerubbabel the son of Shealtiel, and Joshua the son of Josedech, the high priest, with all the remnant of the people, obeyed the voice of the LORD their God, and the words of Haggai the prophet, as the LORD their God had sent him, and the people did fear before the LORD.

Then spake Haggai the LORD's messenger in the LORD's message unto the people, saying, I am with you, saith the LORD.

And the LORD stirred up the spirit of Zerubbabel the son of Shealtiel, governor of Judah, and the spirit of Joshua the son of Josedech, the high priest, and the spirit of all the remnant of the people; and they came and did work in the house of the LORD of hosts, their God,

In the four and twentieth day of the sixth month, in the second year of Darius the king. Haggai 1:1-15.

The Order to Rebuild the Temple

We now have the date: the 24th day of the sixth month of the year 422 BC. On this date, Darius II issued the following decree as set forth in the book of Ezra:

> Then Darius the king made a decree, and search was made in the house of the rolls, where the treasures were laid up in Babylon.
>
> And there was found at Achmetha, in the palace that is in the province of the Medes, a roll, and therein was a record thus written:
>
>> In the first year of Cyrus the king the same Cyrus the king made a decree concerning the house of God at Jerusalem, Let the house be builded, the place where they offered sacrifices, and let the foundations thereof be strongly laid; the height thereof threescore cubits, and the

breadth thereof threescore cubits;

With three rows of great stones, and a row of new timber: and let the expenses be given out of the king's house:

And also let the golden and silver vessels of the house of God, which Nebuchadnezzar took forth out of the temple which is at Jerusalem, and brought unto Babylon, be restored, and brought again unto the temple which is at Jerusalem, every one to his place, and place them in the house of God.

Now therefore, Tatnai, governor beyond the river, Shetharboznai, and your companions the Apharsachites, which are beyond the river, be ye far from thence:

Let the work of this house of God alone; let the governor of the Jews

and the elders of the Jews build this
house of God in his place.

Moreover I make a decree what
ye shall do to the elders of these Jews
for the building of this house of God:
that of the king's goods, even of the
tribute beyond the river, forthwith
expenses be given unto these men,
that they be not hindered.

And that which they have need
of, both young bullocks, and rams, and
lambs, for the burnt offerings of the
God of heaven, wheat, salt, wine, and
oil, according to the appointment of
the priests which are at Jerusalem, let
it be given them day by day without
fail:

That they may offer sacrifices
of sweet savours unto the God of
heaven, and pray for the life of the
king, and of his sons.

Also I have made a decree, that
whosoever shall alter this word, let
timber be pulled down from his house,

and being set up, let him be hanged thereon; and let his house be made a dunghill for this.

And the God that hath caused his name to dwell there destroy all kings and people, that shall put to their hand to alter and to destroy this house of God which is at Jerusalem. I Darius have made a decree; let it be done with speed.

Then Tatnai, governor on this side of the river, Shetharboznai, and their companions, according to that which Darius the king had sent, so they did speedily.

And the elders of the Jews builded, and they prospered through the prophesying of Haggai the prophet and Zechariah the son of Iddo. And they builded, and finished it, according to the commandment of the God of Israel, and according to the commandment of Cyrus, and Darius, and Artaxerxes king of Persia.

And this house was finished on the third day of the month Adar, which was in the sixth year of the reign of Darius the king. Ezra 6:1-15.

The book of Ezra contains the exact wording of the record – the transcript of the legal edicts in force and effect at that time - which set in motion the rebuilding of the temple. Both Ezra and Haggai give us the date: the four and twentieth day of the sixth month, in the second year of Darius the king.

You will need this date as a reference as we discuss the prophecy in the book of Daniel. It is believed that the year of the command was 422 BC.

The Command to Rebuild Jerusalem

Let us now consider the date of the command to rebuild not just the temple, but Jerusalem itself. The date of this command is set forth with particularity in the book of

Nehemiah, chapter 2.

> And it came to pass in the
> month Nisan, in the twentieth year of
> Artaxerxes the king, that wine was
> before him: and I took up the wine,
> and gave it unto the king. Now I had
> not been beforetime sad in his
> presence.

> Wherefore the king said unto
> me, Why is thy countenance sad,
> seeing thou art not sick? this is
> nothing else but sorrow of heart. Then
> I was very sore afraid,

> And said unto the king, Let the
> king live for ever: why should not my
> countenance be sad, when the city, the
> place of my fathers' sepulchres, lieth
> waste, and the gates thereof are
> consumed with fire?

> Then the king said unto me, For
> what dost thou make request? So I
> prayed to the God of heaven.

And I said unto the king, If it please the king, and if thy servant have found favour in thy sight, that thou wouldest send me unto Judah, unto the city of my fathers' sepulchres, that I may build it.

And the king said unto me, (the queen also sitting by him,) For how long shall thy journey be? and when wilt thou return? So it pleased the king to send me; and I set him a time.

Moreover I said unto the king, If it please the king, let letters be given me to the governors beyond the river, that they may convey me over till I come into Judah;

And a letter unto Asaph the keeper of the king's forest, that he may give me timber to make beams for the gates of the palace which appertained to the house, and for the wall of the city, and for the house that I shall enter into. **And the king granted me, according to the good**

hand of my God upon me. Nehemiah
2:1-8.

Artaxerxes had obtained the throne in
465 BC. Nehemiah specifies that the granting
of his request to rebuild the city of his
fathers' sepulcheres (Jerusalem), the palace
and the wall of the city took place in the 20th
year of the reign of Artaxerxes, or 444 BC, 23
years before the command of Darius II to
finish the temple.

It is of some importance that
Nehemiah never disclosed to Artaxerxes that
the city in question was actually Jerusalem.
Nehemiah simply described the city as a city
in Judah, the city of Nehemiah's fathers'
sepulchers.

The first command given to rebuild
Jerusalem was therefore given in 444 BC, one
of the most prophetically important dates in

all of human history: 444 BC. We will see the relevance of this date as we explore the prophecy of Daniel. However, this was the first command to rebuild Jerusalem.

There has been a second command to restore and build Jerusalem, even more explicit than the first. We shall also look at its application.

CHAPTER TWO

The Transgression

With this history behind us, we now embark into prophecy, beginning with Daniel's seventy weeks, a challenge to say the least. Let us consider Daniel 9.

The Date

In the first year of Darius the son of Ahasuerus, of the seed of the Medes, which was made king over the realm of the Chaldeans;

In the first year of his reign I Daniel understood by books the number of the years, whereof the word of the LORD came to Jeremiah the prophet, that he would accomplish seventy years in the desolations of Jerusalem.

This passage contradicts other historians in claiming that Darius, the son of Ahasuerus (Xerxes I), actually held the throne before Artaxerxes I, who murdered Darius around 465 BC. This passage was then given to Daniel in 466-465 BC, and specifies that seventy years of desolations of Jerusalem would be accomplished.

The Captivity

Daniel begins with a date:

> In the third year of the reign of Jehoiakim king of Judah came Nebuchadnezzar king of Babylon unto Jerusalem, and besieged it.
>
> And the Lord gave Jehoiakim king of Judah into his hand, with part of the vessels of the house of God: which he carried into the land of Shinar to the house of his god; and he brought the vessels into the treasure house of his god. Daniel 1:1-2.

Jehoiakim took the throne at the age of twenty-five, 2 Kings 23.36, and reigned for eleven years between 609 and 598 BC. The captivity began then, in 606 BC, and ended three years following the edict of Cyrus the Great in 539 BC – a seventy year captivity.

Jeremiah tells us that this captivity was because of the transgression of Israel:

> The priests said not, Where is the LORD? and they that handle the law knew me not: the pastors also transgressed against me, and the prophets prophesied by Baal, and walked after things that do not profit. Jeremiah 2:8.

> Wherefore will ye plead with me? ye all have transgressed against me, saith the LORD. Jeremiah 2:29.

Consider now the prayer of Daniel found in Daniel 9:

And I set my face unto the Lord God, to seek by prayer and supplications, with fasting, and sackcloth, and ashes:

And I prayed unto the LORD my God, and made my confession, and said, O Lord, the great and dreadful God, keeping the covenant and mercy to them that love him, and to them that keep his commandments;

We have sinned, and have committed iniquity, and have done wickedly, and have rebelled, even by departing from thy precepts and from thy judgments:

Neither have we hearkened unto thy servants the prophets, which spake in thy name to our kings, our princes, and our fathers, and to all the people of the land.

O LORD, righteousness belongeth unto thee, but unto us confusion of faces, as at this day; to the men of Judah, and to the inhabitants of Jerusalem, and unto all Israel, that are near, and that are far off, through all the countries whither thou hast driven them, **because of their trespass that they have trespassed against thee**.

O Lord, to us belongeth confusion of face, to our kings, to our princes, and to our fathers, because we have sinned against thee.

To the Lord our God belong mercies and forgivenesses, though we have rebelled against him;

Neither have we obeyed the voice of the LORD our God, to walk in his laws, which he set before us by his servants the prophets.

Yea, **all Israel have transgressed thy law**, even by departing, that they might not obey thy voice; therefore the curse is poured upon us, and the oath that is written in the law of Moses[1] the servant of God, because we have sinned against him.

And he hath confirmed his words, which he spake against us, and against our judges that judged us, by bringing upon us a great evil: for under the whole heaven hath not been done as hath been done upon Jerusalem.

As it is written in the law of Moses[2], all this evil is come upon us: yet made we not our prayer before the LORD our God, that we might turn from our iniquities, and understand thy truth.

Therefore hath the LORD watched upon the evil, and brought it upon us: for the LORD our God is righteous in all his works which he doeth: for we obeyed not his voice.

---

[1] We will consider this later in more detail.
[2] Deuteronomy 28:15-68.

And now, O Lord our God, that hast brought thy people forth out of the land of Egypt with a mighty hand, and hast gotten thee renown, as at this day; we have sinned, we have done wickedly.

O LORD, according to all thy righteousness, I beseech thee, let thine anger and thy fury be turned away from thy city Jerusalem, thy holy mountain: because for our sins, and for the iniquities of our fathers, Jerusalem and thy people are become a reproach to all that are about us.

Now therefore, O our God, hear the prayer of thy servant, and his supplications, and cause thy face to shine upon thy sanctuary that is desolate, for the Lord's sake.

O my God, incline thine ear, and hear; open thine eyes, and behold our desolations, and the city which is called by thy name: for we do not present our supplications before thee for our righteousnesses, but for thy great mercies.

O Lord, hear; O Lord, forgive; O Lord, hearken and do; defer not, for thine own sake, O my God: for thy city and thy people are called by thy name. Daniel 9:3-19.

One of the curses referred to by Daniel is the curse that is found is Leviticus 26:14-46. This curse, a summary of sorts, reflects the curse in Deuteronomy 28, yet includes prophecy concerning the restoration of Jacob, Isaac and Abraham.

And if ye will not for all this hearken unto me, but walk contrary unto me;

Then I will walk contrary unto you also in fury; and I, even I, will chastise you **seven times** for your sins.

And ye shall eat the flesh of your sons, and the flesh of your daughters shall ye eat.

And I will destroy your high places, and cut down your images, and cast your carcases upon the carcases of your idols, and my soul shall abhor you.

And I will make your cities waste, and bring your sanctuaries unto desolation, and I will not smell the savour of your sweet odours.

And I will bring the land into desolation: and your enemies which dwell therein shall be astonished at it.

And I will scatter you among the heathen, and will draw out a sword after you: and your land shall be desolate, and your cities waste.

Then shall the land enjoy her sabbaths, as long as it lieth desolate, and ye be in your enemies' land; even then shall the land rest, and enjoy her sabbaths.

As long as it lieth desolate it shall rest; because it did not rest in your sabbaths, when ye dwelt upon it.

And upon them that are left alive of you I will send a faintness into their hearts in the lands of their enemies; and the sound of a shaken leaf shall chase them; and they shall flee, as fleeing from a sword; and they shall fall when none pursueth.

And they shall fall one upon another, as it were before a sword, when none pursueth: and ye shall have no power to stand before your enemies.

And ye shall perish among the heathen, and the land of your enemies shall eat you up.

And they that are left of you shall pine away in their iniquity in your enemies' lands; and also in the iniquities of their fathers shall they pine away with them.

If they shall confess their iniquity, and the iniquity of their fathers, with their trespass which they trespassed against me, and that also they have walked contrary unto me;

And that I also have walked contrary unto them, and have brought them into the land of their enemies; if then their uncircumcised hearts be humbled, and they then accept of the punishment of their iniquity:

Then will I remember my covenant with Jacob, and also my covenant with Isaac, and also my covenant with Abraham will I remember; and I will remember the land.

The land also shall be left of them, and shall enjoy her sabbaths, while she lieth desolate without them: and they shall accept of the punishment of their iniquity: because, even because they despised my judgments, and because their soul abhorred my statutes.

And yet for all that, when they be in the land of their enemies, I will not cast them away, neither will I abhor them, to destroy them utterly, and to break my covenant with them: for I am the LORD their God.

But I will for their sakes remember the covenant of their ancestors, whom I brought forth out of the land of Egypt in the sight of the heathen, that I might be their God: I am the LORD. Leviticus 26:27-45.

This is but one part of the curse set forth in Leviticus 26, but in the case of the captivity in Babylon, this was the operative part. The land was given Sabbath, seventy years of Sabbath, and the people of Israel were taken away into foreign lands.

A concise history of the workings of this curse is found in 2 Chronicles.

The Transgression

Zedekiah was one and twenty years old when he began to reign, and reigned eleven years in Jerusalem.

And he did that which was evil in the sight of the LORD his God, and humbled not himself before Jeremiah the prophet speaking from the mouth of the LORD.

And he also rebelled against king Nebuchadnezzar, who had made him swear by God: but he stiffened his neck, and hardened his heart from turning unto the LORD God of Israel.

Moreover all the chief of the priests, and the people, **transgressed very much after all the abominations of the heathen**; and polluted the house of the LORD which he had hallowed in Jerusalem.

And the LORD God of their fathers sent to them by his messengers, rising up betimes, and sending; because he had compassion on his people, and on his dwelling place:

But they mocked the messengers of God, and despised his words, and misused his prophets, until the wrath of the LORD arose against his people, till there was no remedy.

The Wrath

Therefore he brought upon them the king of the Chaldees, who slew their young men with the sword in the house of their sanctuary, and had no compassion upon young man or maiden, old man, or him that stooped for age: he gave them all into his hand.

And all the vessels of the house of God, great and small, and the treasures of the house of the LORD, and the treasures of the king, and of his princes; all these he brought to Babylon.

And they burnt the house of God, and brake down the wall of Jerusalem, and burnt all the palaces thereof with fire, and destroyed all the goodly vessels thereof.

And them that had escaped from the sword carried he away to Babylon; where they were servants to him and his sons until the reign of the kingdom of Persia:

The Land Enjoys Its Sabbath

To fulfil the word of the LORD by the mouth of Jeremiah, until the land had enjoyed her sabbaths: for as long as she lay desolate she kept sabbath, to fulfil threescore and ten years.

The Cyrus Decree Ending Captivity

Now in the first year of Cyrus king of Persia, that the word of the LORD spoken by the mouth of Jeremiah might be accomplished, the LORD stirred up the spirit of Cyrus king of Persia, that he made a proclamation throughout all his kingdom, and put it also in writing, saying,

Thus saith Cyrus king of Persia, All the kingdoms of the earth hath the LORD God of heaven given me; and he hath charged me to build him an house in Jerusalem, which is in Judah. Who is there among you of all his people? The LORD his God be with him, and let him go up.

Because of Daniel's prayer and in accordance with the will of God as prophesized, Judea was restored: the covenant was restored; the land enjoyed its Sabbaths; when they were in the land of their enemies, they were not destroyed. This was done to restore the relationship of chosen with their God.

The Curse Today

Before we leave, let's take a look at the rest of the curse, and see if it has any applicability today:

> 16I also will do this unto you; I will even **appoint over you terror**, consumption, and the burning ague, that shall consume the eyes, and cause sorrow of heart: and ye shall sow your seed in vain, for your enemies shall eat it.

Has terror been appointed over our nation? We remain with armies in foreign lands, and we still take off our shoes at the airport. Terrorism has been initiated against us such that we have declared war on it.

17And I will set my face against you, and ye shall be slain before your enemies: **they that hate you shall reign over you**; and **ye shall flee when none pursueth you**.

Seven years following the single largest loss of civilian life in American history when Muslim terrorists attacked and destroyed the twin towers in New York, we went ahead and elected as our President a Muslim leader with the middle name of our adversary in Iraq – Hussein – and the last name (in Swahili) of our adversary who was leading al Qaeda – Obama (Swahili for Usama or Osama). Have we not fled from an adversary who has not pursued us?

18And if ye will not yet for all this hearken unto me, then I will punish you seven times more for your sins.

This sounds like there is more to
come.

> [19]And I will break the pride of your
> power; and I will make your heaven as
> iron, and your earth as brass:

We now have a President who has
apologized for the "pride of our power" all
over the world, even to those enemies who
have sworn our destruction. Now ask
yourself if our heaven is as iron and our earth
as brass. Begin by asking those farming in
the San Joaquin valley in California.

> [20]And your strength shall be spent in
> vain: for your land shall not yield her
> increase, neither shall the trees of the
> land yield their fruits.

How many billions have been spent in

Iraq?

What has been the success? How
many billions have been spent in

Afghanistan? What has been the success?
How many American lives have been lost in
Iraq and Afghanistan? What fruits have been
yielded from these endeavors? Have we not
spent our strength in vain?

> [21]And if ye walk contrary unto me,
> and will not hearken unto me; I will
> bring seven times more plagues upon
> you according to your sins.

This sounds like there is more to
come, but this has a special connotation: this
includes a seven-fold retribution "according
to your sins." This might be a terrifying
prospect, given 50 million Americans who
never saw the light of day, due to the carnage
of abortion. At a minimum, 50 million
Americans may not be able to avoid
extermination on the basis of convenience.
Woe to us should that continue "seven times".

²²I will also send wild beasts among you, which shall rob you of your children, and destroy your cattle, and make you few in number; and your high ways shall be desolate.

This is an interesting part of the curse. A little research indicates that wolves are now be repatriated in the US, packs of which are now killing cattle.[3] Bears are on the

---

[3] After the U. S. Endangered Species Act of 1973 protected the wolf in the 48 contiguous United States as of 1974 and public attitudes about wolves improved, wolves began to colonize a wide variety of habitats and to demonstrate that they did not require wilderness. The wolf has now begun to recover in the northern U. S. and in several parts of Europe. The question of the next decade will not be how to save the wolf, but rather how best to manage the animal. *David Mech, David L.,* **The Challenge and Opportunity of Recovering Wolf Populations,** *Conservation Biology*; 1995. 9(2): 1-9.

rebound;[4] snakes are dramatically increasing and appearing in areas of the United States where they have never been seen before;[5] and consider the infestation of African killer bees[6] and the rise of locusts in Nevada and

---

[4] Bombey, Nancy, **Bear population booms, aim is to lessen encounters, Citizen-Times.com, Oct. 18, 2009,** http://www.citizen-times.com/article/20091018/NEWS01/910180354/Bear-population-booms--aim-is-to-lessen-encounters

[5] Thousands of really big non-native snakes — we're talking boa constrictors, anacondas and pythons — slither wild in southern Florida. And there's nothing holding them in the Sunshine State. Which is why a report that was released today contends they pose moderate to high ecological threats to states on three U.S. coasts. Raloff, Janet, Giant Snakes Warming to U.S. Climes,Oct. 13, 2009, http://www.sciencenews.org/view/generic/id/48392/title/Science_%2B_the_Public_Giant_snakes_warming_to_U.S._climes

[6] Africanized honeybees, a hybrid species of docile European honeybees and a more violent southern African strain, are extremely dangerous. Accidently released in Brazil in 1957, the bees slowly migrated northward, reaching Arizona by 1993. The aggressive

Arizona.[7] Given the dramatically rising cost
of oil, how long will it be until our highways
will be desolate.

>[23]And if ye will not be reformed by
>me by these things, but will walk
>contrary unto me;

>[24]Then will I also walk contrary unto
>you, and will punish you yet seven
>times for your sins.

>[25]And I will bring a sword upon you,
>that shall avenge the quarrel of my
>covenant: and when ye are gathered
>together within your cities, I will send

---

bees attack if provoked, follow people for over a mile,
and sting a lot. Green, Stewart, Killer Bees Attack
Arizona Climber, About.com, Sept. 16, 2009.
http://climbing.about.com/b/2009/09/16/killer-
bees-attack-arizona-climber.htm

[7] Jim Carlton (April 24, 2009). "Against Insect Plague,
Nevadans Wield Ultimate Weapon: Hard Rock". Wall
Street Journal.
http://online.wsj.com/article/SB1240521128502496
91.html#mod=rss_whats_news_us.

the pestilence among you; and ye shall
be delivered into the hand of the
enemy.

Although there are no attacking
armies on US soil (yet), the pestilence most
certainly appears to be among us, from
Australian hepatitis to H1N1. We have not
yet been delivered into the hand of the
enemy – at least the enemy foreign. It most
certainly appears, though, that we have been
delivered into the hands of the enemy within.

> 26And when I have broken the staff of
> your bread, ten women shall bake
> your bread in one oven, and they shall
> deliver you your bread again by
> weight: and ye shall eat, and not be
> satisfied.

This food scarcity has not yet come
about, but see Behold! A Black Horse! by this
author.

27And if ye will not for all this hearken unto me, but walk contrary unto me;

28Then I will walk contrary unto you also in fury; and I, even I, will chastise you seven times for your sins.

29And ye shall eat the flesh of your sons, and the flesh of your daughters shall ye eat.

This has not yet come about.

30And I will destroy your high places, and cut down your images, and cast your carcases upon the carcases of your idols, and my soul shall abhor you.

This has not yet come about.

31And I will make your cities waste, and bring your sanctuaries unto desolation, and I will not smell the savour of your sweet odours.

This has not yet come about.

³²And I will bring the land into desolation: and your enemies which dwell therein shall be astonished at it.

This has not yet come about.

³³And I will scatter you among the heathen, and will draw out a sword after you: and your land shall be desolate, and your cities waste.

This has not yet come about.   It makes one wonder what could bring about such a transgression.

CHAPTER THREE

Daniel's Seventy Weeks

It was during the course of this prayer, that Daniel is given a vision by the angle Gabriel of seventy weeks, to wit:

The Prophecy

Seventy weeks are determined upon thy people and upon thy holy city, to finish the transgression, and to make an end of sins, and to make reconciliation for iniquity, and to bring in everlasting righteousness, and to seal up the vision and prophecy, and to anoint the most Holy.

Know therefore and understand, that from the going forth of the commandment to restore and to build Jerusalem unto the Messiah the Prince shall be seven weeks, and threescore and two weeks: the street shall be built again, and the wall, even in troublous times.

And after threescore and two weeks shall Messiah be cut off, but not for himself: and the people of the prince that shall come shall destroy the city and the sanctuary; and the end thereof shall be with a flood, and unto the end of the war desolations are determined.

And he shall confirm the covenant with many for one week: and in the midst of the week he shall cause the sacrifice and the oblation to cease, and for the overspreading of abominations he shall make it desolate, even until the consummation, and that determined shall be poured upon the desolate.

This prophecy has presented a challenge to all who have attempted an analysis. Nonetheless, let us now consider this prophecy piece by piece. The phrase "seventy weeks" was translated from the Hebrew word Shabuwa, which means both a period of seven days, and also the feast of weeks (Shavuot or Pentacost).

So, initially, the question is: what is meant by "seventy weeks"? A literal understanding would mean that the transgression was finished in a year-and-a-half, an end of sins was made in a year-and-a-half, iniquity was reconciled, righteousness was made everlasting, vision and prophecy were sealed, and the most Holy was anointed. The Sabbath for the land began in 606 BC, so if this is to be taken literally, the transgression was over in 605 BC. Historically, this is impossible, and the Hebrew term Shabuwa gives us an inclination.

Because Shabuwa has two meanings – a period of seven days, and a reference to the feast of weeks, we have two constructions to the prophecy.

> "Seventy feasts of weeks are determined upon thy people and upon thy holy city, to finish the transgression, and to make an end of sins, and to make reconciliation for iniquity, . . .

In the use, the prophecy concerns seventy years – seventy feasts of weeks. Consider then that Daniel's prophecy proclaims that seventy years would be the length of the captivity, that seventy years would bring an end to the desolation imposed on Jerusalem, that seventy years would finish the transgression that was found under the reign of Zedikiah, that seventy years would be the end of the sins creating this desolation, and seventy years to make reconciliation for this iniquity.

The second half of this prophecy is a setting of the stage for the second understanding. Seventy years, the rebuilding of Jerusalem, the temple, and the wall, will create circumstance that will "bring in everlasting righteousness," which will "seal up the vision and prophecy, and which will "anoint the most Holy".

A Day Equals A Year

> After the number of the days in which ye searched the land, even forty days, **each day for a year**, shall ye bear your iniquities, even forty years, and ye shall know my breach of promise. Numbers 14:34.

Where prophecy concerning the captivity and that period following captivity is concerned, Ezekiel proclaims that a similar equalization is present.

Lie thou also upon thy left side, and lay the iniquity of the house of Israel upon it: according to the number of the days that thou shalt lie upon it thou shalt bear their iniquity.

For **I have laid upon thee the years of their iniquity, according to the number of the days, three hundred and ninety days**: so shalt thou bear the iniquity of the house of Israel.

And when thou hast accomplished them, lie again on thy right side, and thou shalt bear the iniquity of the house of Judah forty days: **I have appointed thee each day for a year.** Ezekiel 4:4-6.

Ezekiel therefore predicts Gentile rule over the land of Israel for 430 years, using the day equals a year formula. Ezekiel begins his prophecy in the fifth year of the captivity of Jehoiachin, or 593 BC. Ezekiel 1:2. He predicts 430 years of domination by the Gentiles, or through 163 BC, during the period when Judas Maccabeus is credited with restoring Judea and restoring worship in the temple in 165 BC. It is worth noting that the second temple was not the temple of the sons of Jacob, but rather the temple of the Judea, built by the Levite clan of the Maccabees.

Let us now consider Daniel's seventy weeks.

> Know therefore and understand, that from the going forth of the commandment to restore and to build Jerusalem unto the Messiah the Prince shall be seven weeks, and threescore and two weeks: the street shall be built again, and the wall, even in troublous times.

There is but one edict to restore and to build Jerusalem, and it is the edict given to

Nehemiah by Ataxerxes I in 445 BC. Because a day equals a year in this prophecy, from 445 BC to thc Messiah shall be seven weeks, or 49 years to 396 BC – the year of the emergence of Aristotle who would later tutor Alexander the Great, the king that would realize Daniel's prophecies beginning in 10:10, and threescore and two weeks, an additional sixty-two weeks or 434 years, which together give us a total of 483 years, which would take us to the year 38 AD.

The Prophetic Calendar

Enter the Essenes. The Essenes were a pious religious group in the Judean area that arose after the Maccabean revolt (167-160 BC). They were a community of people who practiced celibacy, baptism and the sharing of wine, and they were isolated from the Pharisees and the Sadducees and consequently the Judean culture because of the practice of a solar calendar. Some scholars believe that both John the Baptist and Jesus practiced Essenian traditions rather than the practices of the Pharisees and the Sadducees. This adjustment to the solar calendar placed all of the Jewish feast days on different days, including the Sabbath.

The key to understanding the prophecies in the book of Daniel is to understand that his references are to a prophetic 360 day year. There are those who hold that at one time, prior to the flood at the time of Noah, the lunar calendar of 360 days was the same length as a solar 360 day year. Consequently, in order to find the calendar year prophesized, an adjustment must be made to the day/year prophecies of Daniel, adjusting by a factor of .9863 (360/365).

Consequently, the number of solar years in Daniel's 69 weeks is 476 years.

Given Artaxerxes edict of 445 BC, the date the Messiah should appear is now 31 AD. The Gospel of Luke tells us that he began His ministry when he was thirty years old (Luke 3:23) upon His baptism. If He was born in the year 1 AD (Anno Domini – the year of our Lord), then he was 1 in the year 2, and 30 years of age, his ministry began in the year 31 AD, and continued for 3½ years, fulfilled by His crucifixion.

Returning to our prophecy, we see this dating three times in Daniel 9:

> Seventy weeks [483 years in this understanding] are determined upon thy people and upon thy holy city, to finish the transgression, and to make an end of sins, and to make reconciliation for iniquity, and to bring in everlasting righteousness,

and to seal up the vision and prophecy, and to anoint the most Holy.

Know therefore and understand, that from the going forth of the commandment to restore and to build Jerusalem [445 BC] unto the Messiah the Prince shall be seven weeks, and threescore and two weeks [476 years]: the street shall be built again, and the wall, even in troublous times [this prophecy is fulfilled in Nehemiah].

And after threescore and two weeks shall Messiah be cut off [sometime after 31 AD], but not for himself: and the people of the prince that shall come [the Roman princes Vaspasian and Titus] shall destroy the city and the sanctuary [70 AD]; and the end thereof shall be with a flood [the Romans killed so many people in Jerusalem, that the running blood actually put out fires], and unto the end of the war desolations are determined.

And he shall confirm the covenant with many for one week [the ministry of Christ was confirmed within 7 years of its beginning in 31 AD]: and in the midst of the week [3½ years into His ministry] he shall cause the sacrifice and the oblation to cease [meaningless after the tearing of the curtain], and for the overspreading of abominations he shall make it desolate, even until the consummation, and that determined shall be poured upon the desolate.

Jesus caused the sacrifice and oblation to cease because of His sacrifice on the cross, which ended the sacrifice once and for all. At the same time, His death on the cross also, for the overspreading abominations, made Jerusalem desolate until the "consummation." At this time, His death on the cross caused that which was determined to be poured upon the desolate [the destruction of Jerusalem, and its desolation for 1,878 years].

Daniels seventy weeks, assuming only one command to rebuild Jerusalem, was therefore fulfilled in the ministry and crucifixion of Christ, and the subsequent destruction of Jerusalem and the Judean kingdom in 70 AD. However, that realization is a realization that contemplates the first meaning of the term "Shabuwa" (sevens).

When the term is construed under the second meaning of the term - "Shavuot or Pentecost" – it is possible to limit the dating to only seventy Shavuots instead of 490, although Pentacost is a feast of sevens – a feast following seven weeks of seven days. Shavuots are annual experiences, whether under the solar or lunar calendar;

consequently, when Shabuwa means Shavuot, we are discussing 70 actual years.

This has its own realization to some degree during the lifetime of Daniel, predicting the number of years of the Babylon captivity in its first instance. We will consider these seventy Shavuot again, when the command to restore and build Jerusalem is once again uttered under the supervisions of the re-birthed Babylon.

CHAPTER FOUR

Daniel's two witnesses for the return
of Babylon

There is an interesting anomaly appearing in the book of Daniel. In Daniel 5, verse 30, Belshazzar the King of the Chaldeans is slain. Yet, Daniel 7, the chapter begins with the phrase "in the first year of Belshazzar, King of Babylon; and Daniel 8 begins with "in the third year of the reign of King Belshazzar. Daniel 5, the chapter detailing the last day in the life of Belshazzar, is conspicuously out of place, if the order of the book is to be chronological.

However, there is another reason why Daniel 5 appears immediately after Daniel 4. The words of Jesus in the gospel of Matthew, which quote Deuteronomy 19:15, tell us that "by the mouth of two or three witnesses every word may be established." A close examination of Daniel 4 and Daniel 5 discloses the testimony of two witnesses to a very interesting fact: the re-emergence of the empire of Babylon. Let's start with the prophetic dating found in Daniel 4.

> Then Daniel, whose name was Belteshazzar, was astonished for one hour, and his thoughts troubled him. The king spake, and said, Belteshazzar, let not the dream, or the interpretation thereof, trouble thee. Belteshazzar answered and said, My lord, the dream be to them that hate thee, and the interpretation thereof to thine enemies.
>
> The tree that thou sawest, which grew, and was strong, whose height reached unto the heaven, and the sight thereof to all the earth;

Whose leaves were fair, and the fruit thereof much, and in it was meat for all; under which the beasts of the field dwelt, and upon whose branches the fowls of the heaven had their habitation:

It is thou, O king, that art grown and become strong: for thy greatness is grown, and reacheth unto heaven, and thy dominion to the end of the earth.

And whereas the king saw a watcher and an holy one coming down from heaven, and saying, Hew the tree down, and destroy it; yet leave the stump of the roots thereof in the earth, even with a band of iron and brass, in the tender grass of the field; and let it be wet with the dew of heaven, and let his portion be with the beasts of the field, till seven times pass over him;

This is the interpretation, O king, and this is the decree of the most

High, which is come upon my lord the king:

That they shall drive thee from men, and thy dwelling shall be with the beasts of the field, and they shall make thee to eat grass as oxen, and they shall wet thee with the dew of heaven, and seven times shall pass over thee, till thou know that the most High ruleth in the kingdom of men, and giveth it to whomsoever he will.

And whereas they commanded to leave the stump of the tree roots; thy kingdom shall be sure unto thee, after that thou shalt have known that the heavens do rule.

-    Daniel 4:19-26

The keys in this passage are the issue of the seven times passing over Nebuchadnezzar, and the restoration of the kingdom following the seven times.

Again, the prophetic year is applicable here to determine how many years we are discussing. Historically, "seven times" did in fact pass over Nebuchadnezzar, as he was outcast for seven years.

Seven prophetic years are seven 360 day years. Seven 360 day years equals 2,520 days total. Since a day is equal to a year (as demonstrated above), we are discussing 2,520 prophetic years. To determine the number of calendar years using our modern solar calendar, we multiply the number of prophetic years by 360 days, and then divide by 365 days. The answer then gives us the actual calendar year.

$$2{,}520 \times 360 \div 365 = 2{,}485$$

The collapse of Babylon occurred on October 13, 539 B.C. We can subtract 539 from 2,485 since there is no year zero. When we do, we find the year predicted for the return of the kingdom of Babylon. The equation is simply 2,488 – 539 = 1946. This passage in Daniel 4 prophesizes that the kingdom of Babylon will be restored in the latter days, specifically in the year 1946. The Arab League, or the League of Arab States, was organized during the year 1945 as World War II wore down and was effectively in place by 1946. The Arab League noticeably includes the former lands of Babylon.

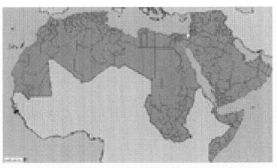

Administrative divisions in the Arab League

Now let us consider Daniel 5.

> Then was the part of the hand
> sent from him; and this writing
> was written.
>
> And this is the writing that was
> written, MENE, MENE, TEKEL,
> UPHARSIN.
>
> This is the interpretation of the
> thing: MENE; God hath
> numbered thy kingdom, and
> finished it.
>
> TEKEL; Thou art weighed in
> the balances, and art found
> wanting.
>
> PERES; Thy kingdom is
> divided, and given to the Medes
> and Persians.
>
> Then commanded Belshazzar,
> and they clothed Daniel with
> scarlet, and put a chain of gold
> about his neck, and made a
> proclamation concerning him,

that he should be the third
ruler in the kingdom.

In that night was Belshazzar
the king of the Chaldeans slain.

– Daniel 5:24-30

Although Daniel defined these three terms prophetically, each word also names a certain amount of money. The MENE (Strong's H4483) (P'al) mina, maneh is defined as a weight of measurement or measurement; usually 50 shekels but maybe 60 shekels. The TEKEL is the same as the SHEKEL. The PERES means the MENE divided, or 25 shekels but maybe 30 shekels. Ezekiel 45:12 tells us the "the shekel shall be twenty gerahs."

Back we go to the calculator to determine if a number emerges. MENE (50 shekels), MENE (50 shekels), TEKEL (1 shekel), PERES (25 shekels) gives us the equation 50 + 50 + 1 + 25 = 126.

Now let us take the total number of shekels – 126 – and multiply by its ultimate reduction – the gerah, which yields the sum . . . 2,520. This is the second time this number has appeared (the first being in Chapter 4). Daniel Chapter 5 is therefore not out of place. It was placed next to Chapter 4 to be a second witness as to this number and its subsequent date.

The witnessing to these 2,520 prophetic years is so important in the book of Daniel, that Daniel takes Chapter 5 out of chronological order to set it aside Daniel 4. Is there any other explanation for this placement? As Daniel stated, the kingdom was divided - - divided in time, by 2,520 prophetic years and 2,485 solar calendar years.

John tells us in Revelation, that there will be another Babylon, a latter day "mystery Babylon":

> I saw a woman sit upon a scarlet coloured beast, full of names of blasphemy, having seven heads and ten horns.
>
> [4]And the woman was arrayed in purple and scarlet colour, and decked with gold and precious stones and pearls, having a golden cup in her hand full of abominations and filthiness of her fornication:
>
> [5]And upon her forehead was a name written, MYSTERY, BABYLON THE GREAT, THE MOTHER OF HARLOTS AND ABOMINATIONS OF THE EARTH.
>
> -   Revelation 17:3-5

Did we see its re-emergence in 1946?

CHAPTER FIVE

Daniel's 1290 days

Daniel's calendar continues with amazing accuracy as he continues to set forth dates, our understanding having been unsealed with the realization of the dating mechanism found in the 360 day prophetic year and its adjustment to the actual year.

Now, let us consider that passage found in Daniel 12:

> And from the time that the daily sacrifice shall be taken away, and the abomination that maketh desolate set up, there shall be a thousand two hundred and ninety days.
> - Daniel 12:11

Daniel specifies that "from the time that the daily sacrifice shall be taken away" until the time that "the abomination that maketh desolate" is set up, there shall be 1,290 days.

Let us begin with our understanding of the prophetic dating set forth previously in Daniel 4, Daniel 5, and Daniel 9. The 1,290 years must be multiplied by 360 prophetic days and then divided by 365 actual days to determine the number of actual calendar years, which in this case is 1,272 years.

Our next step is to find out what was the time that the daily sacrifice was "taken away".

> And in the fifth month, on the seventh day of the month, which is the nineteenth year of king Nebuchadnezzar king of Babylon, came Nebuzaradan, captain of the guard, a servant of the king of Babylon, unto Jerusalem:
>
> And he burnt the house of the LORD, and the king's house, and all the

houses of Jerusalem, and every great man's house burnt he with fire.

And all the army of the Chaldees, that were with the captain of the guard, brake down the walls of Jerusalem round about.

Now the rest of the people that were left in the city, and the fugitives that fell away to the king of Babylon, with the remnant of the multitude, did Nebuzaradan the captain of the guard carry away.

But the captain of the guard left of the poor of the land to be vinedressers and husbandmen.

And the pillars of brass that were in the house of the LORD, and the bases, and the brasen sea that was in the house of the LORD, did the Chaldees break in pieces, and carried the brass of them to Babylon.

And the pots, and the shovels, and the snuffers, and the spoons, and all the

vessels of brass wherewith they
ministered, took they away.

And the firepans, and the bowls, and
such things as were of gold, in gold,
and of silver, in silver, the captain of
the guard took away.

The two pillars, one sea, and the bases
which Solomon had made for the
house of the LORD; the brass of all
these vessels was without weight.

The height of the one pillar was
eighteen cubits, and the chapiter upon
it was brass: and the height of the
chapiter three cubits; and the
wreathen work, and pomegranates
upon the chapiter round about, all of
brass: and like unto these had the
second pillar with wreathen work.

And the captain of the guard *took
Seraiah the chief priest, and Zephaniah
the second priest, and the three keepers
of the door*:

- 2 Kings 25:8-18

The nineteenth year of Nebuchadnezzar was the year that the last Levite priests and the very last remnants of the temple were taken away (and the context is that they were taken, not destroyed or prohibited). This famous king of Babylon reigned from 603 B.C. to 562 B.C., so his 19th year was 584 B.C. When we calculate the 1,272 years from the date that the daily sacrifice was taken away, we arrive at the year 688 A.D. This date was the date when the "abomination that maketh desolate" was prophesized to appear.

It is of some note that the construction of the Dome of the Rock began in 688 A.D and was completed in 691 A.D. This building is the very first building of Islam and is built in that area of the temple mount in Jerusalem now identified as the outer court of the original temple.

Inside the building in classical Arabic is inscribed, "O you People of the Book, overstep not bounds in your religion, and of God speak only the truth. The Messiah, Jesus, son of Mary, is only an apostle of God, and his Word which he conveyed unto Mary, and a Spirit proceeding from him. Believe therefore in God and his apostles, and say not Three. It will be better for you. God is only one God. Far be it from his glory that he should have a son."

There are two keys of understanding in this statement: First, the apostolic ministry of Christ is claimed to be only to convey his Word *unto Mary*. Second, Islam denies that God has *a son*. Let us determine if this denunciation of the deity of Christ is the "abomination that maketh desolate" referred to in Daniel.

CHAPTER SIX

Revelation's two witnesses

As we review the timing set forth in scripture, we must ask ourselves whether the hermeneutic making a day equal a year found in Ezekiel and Daniel continues without abatement into Revelation. The prophecies of Daniel cannot be understood unless the days referred to in Daniel 9 and Daniel 12 are equal to years – the day equals a year formula. Daniel carries with it the additional understanding of the prophetic, 360 day year.

Many commentators believe that the days set forth in Revelation mean merely days, yet we have a direct tie between Daniel and Revelation. Consider this prophecy concerning the Antichrist found in Daniel 7:

²³Thus he said, The fourth beast shall be the fourth kingdom upon earth, which shall be diverse from all kingdoms, and shall devour the whole earth, and shall tread it down, and break it in pieces.

²⁴And the ten horns out of this kingdom are ten kings that shall arise: and another shall rise after them; and he shall be diverse from the first, and he shall subdue three kings.

²⁵And he shall speak great words against the most High, and shall wear out the saints of the most High, and think to change times and laws: and they shall be given into his hand until a time and times and the dividing of time.

²⁶But the judgment shall sit, and they shall take away his dominion, to consume and to destroy it unto the end.

²⁷And the kingdom and dominion, and the greatness of the kingdom

under the whole heaven, shall be
given to the people of the saints of the
most High, whose kingdom is an
everlasting kingdom, and all
dominions shall serve and obey him.

28Hitherto is the end of the matter. As
for me Daniel, my cogitations much
troubled me, and my countenance
changed in me: but I kept the matter
in my heart.   -
Daniel 7:23-28

Let us then consider the passage "and

they shall be given into his hand until a time

and times and the dividing of time," found in

Daniel and its corollary found in Revelation

12:

13And when the dragon saw that he
was cast unto the earth, he persecuted
the woman which brought forth the
man child.

14And to the woman were given two
wings of a great eagle, that she might

fly into the wilderness, into her place, where she is nourished for a time, and times, and half a time, from the face of the serpent.

-   Revelation 12:13-14

We can consider "times" as they have been previously established in the book of Daniel. Daniel 4 tells us that Nebuchadnezzar's heart would be changed from man's, and a beast's heart would be given unto him; and "seven times" would pass over him.   We know this historically to be seven years. Since a time equals a year when the term first appears in Daniel, and Revelation then gives us "a time, and times, and half a time" reflecting "a time and times and dividing of time" found in Daniel. In short, let us conclude that a "time" is equal to a year.

Therefore, a time, times and half a time is equal to a year, years, and a half a year. This carries with it a bit of ambiguity, since it does clarify that years is only two years. A plain reading appears to mean at a minimum two years or more years. In addition, in Daniel we may or may not have one half year, having "time and times and the dividing of time." Interpreting this where a time equals a year, the read is a "year and years and the dividing of a year," telling us that the measurement is at least 3 years or more, with an add-on of something less than a year.

Most interpreters give us the same dating for both passages; claiming that the time, times and dividing of or half a time equals three and a half years. In the case of Daniel, that would be three and a half prophetic years, while in Revelation, we are discussing three and a half calendar years. There is a difference.

Three and a half prophetic years would yield a total of 1,260 days, whereas three and a half calendar years would yield a total of 1,277.5 days. Once again, because of this correlation between Daniel and Revelation, we construe each day to equal a year. This analysis yields interesting results. Consider Revelation 11:

> And there was given me a reed like unto a rod: and the angel stood, saying, Rise, and measure the temple of God, and the altar, and them that worship therein.

> But the court which is without the temple leave out, and measure it not; for it is given unto the Gentiles: and

the holy city shall they tread under foot forty and two months.

And I will give power unto my two witnesses, and they shall prophesy a thousand two hundred and threescore days, clothed in sackcloth.

These are the two olive trees, and the two candlesticks standing before the God of the earth.

And if any man will hurt them, fire proceedeth out of their mouth, and devoureth their enemies: and if any man will hurt them, he must in this manner be killed.

These have power to shut heaven, that it rain not in the days of their prophecy: and have power over waters to turn them to blood, and to smite the earth with all plagues, as often as they will.

And when they shall have finished their testimony, the beast that ascendeth out of the bottomless pit shall make war against them, and shall overcome them, and kill them.

And their dead bodies shall lie in the street of the great city, which spiritually is called Sodom and Egypt, where also our Lord was crucified. -Revelation 11:1-8

This passage has two datelines: 1) forty-two months; and 2) 1,260 days (3 -1/2 prophetic years). When a day equals a year, 42 months equals 1,277.5 days, the same number as our time, times and half a time. This 42 month period is the time in which the Gentiles tread the holy city under foot. There can be no question that the holy city is Jerusalem. From some point, the Gentiles will trample Jerusalem for 1, 277.5 years.

As we have seen from the last chapter, the Gentiles began to trample the holy city underfoot when the reign of the Gentiles was established over the city following the conquest of the city in 638 A.D. The trampling did not begin until construction began on the Dome of the Rock in 688 A.D. This is not pulling a text out of context to reach a point. This construction point is established as predicted in Daniel 12, when the abomination that maketh desolate is set up. Of course, it took three years (688 – 691) to build the shrine (it was built on Roman foundations), the median point being 689.5 years. If the trampling began at the median point and continued for 42 months (1,277.5 years), you would expect the control of the holy city to be restored to non-Gentiles. This analysis provides us with the year 1967 for the date that the trampling of the holy city would end. This is the year that the nation of

Israel recaptured the city of Jerusalem in the
Six Day War.

Again, as we consider the other date in
Revelation 11 – 1,260 days – we should mark
from the date that the abomination that
maketh desolate is set up (688 A.D.) to
determine when the two witnesses would be
empowered to prophecy. The dating here
appears to be from 688 A.D. until 1948, the
year of the formation of the nation of Israel.

> And I will give power unto my two
> witnesses, and they shall prophesy a
> thousand two hundred and threescore
> days, clothed in sackcloth.
>
> These are the two olive trees, and the
> two candlesticks standing before the
> God of the earth.
>
> And if any man will hurt them, fire
> proceedeth out of their mouth, and
> devoureth their enemies: and if any

man will hurt them, he must in this manner be killed.

These have power to shut heaven, that it rain not in the days of their prophecy: and have power over waters to turn them to blood, and to smite the earth with all plagues, as often as they will.

And when they shall have finished their testimony, the beast that ascendeth out of the bottomless pit shall make war against them, and shall overcome them, and kill them.

And their dead bodies shall lie in the street of the great city, which spiritually is called Sodom and Egypt, where also our Lord was crucified.

CHAPTER SEVEN

Of the seven trumpets, one through four

One question that must be asked is whether timing can be discovered from the text of the book of Revelation as to when the *Antichrist* might be expected. Let us consider Revelation 8.

Revelation 8

> ¹And when he had opened the seventh seal, there was silence in heaven about the space of half an hour.
>
> ²And I saw the seven angels which stood before God; and to them were given seven trumpets.
>
> ³And another angel came and stood at the altar, having a golden censer; and there was given unto him much

incense, that he should offer it with the prayers of all saints upon the golden altar which was before the throne.

4And the smoke of the incense, which came with the prayers of the saints, ascended up before God out of the angel's hand.

5And the angel took the censer, and filled it with fire of the altar, and cast it into the earth: and there were voices, and thunderings, and lightnings, and an earthquake.

-   Revelation 8:1-5

Is there evidence of an earthquake of consequence in biblical history? Absolutely. This means that the date of this earthquake is something that can be discovered. Consider the discussion in Amos 1:

1The words of Amos, who was among the herdmen of Tekoa, which he saw

concerning Israel in the days of Uzziah
king of Judah, and in the days of
Jeroboam the son of Joash king of
Israel, two years before the
earthquake.

-Amos 1:1

Amos was given this prophecy two
years before the earthquake. This date of this
earthquake is something which can be
discovered. Geologists Steven Austin, Gordon
Franz and Eric Frost have found evidence of a
large earthquake in the 7.8 to 8.2 magnitude
that occurred in Israel around 760 B.C.[8]

The reign of Uzziah over Judah began
in 768/767 B.C. and reigned for fifty-two
years. Jeroboam, son of Jehoash, began his

---

[8] Steven A. Austin, Gordon W. Franz, and Eric G. Frost,
"Amos's Earthquake: An Extraordinary Middle East
Seismic Event of 750 B.C." *International Geology
Review* 42 (2000) 657-671.

co-regency over Israel (the northern kingdom) with his father in 793/792, became sole regent in 782/781 and died in the fall of 753 B.C. The window that occurs between the two regents is therefore 768/767 – 753 B.C. It appears as though the date of 760 B.C. is a close approximation.

The seven trumpets therefore prepare to sound beginning in 760 B.C., a marker showing that the wrath of God is about to occur against the house of Jacob.

> 6And the seven angels which had the seven trumpets prepared themselves to sound.
>
> 7The first angel sounded, and there followed hail and fire mingled with blood, and they were cast upon the earth: and the third part of trees was burnt up, and all green grass was burnt up.

-    Revelation 8:6-7

Hail and fire are found in one other place in scripture: Isaiah 30:30. In this passage, Isaiah announces a prophecy against Assyria which most certainly takes place.

> [30]And the LORD shall cause his glorious voice to be heard, and shall shew the lighting down of his arm, with the indignation of his anger, and with the flame of a devouring fire, with scattering, and tempest, and hailstones.
>
> [31]For through the voice of the LORD shall the Assyrian be beaten down, which smote with a rod.

-    Isaiah 30:30-31

In 607/606 B.C., Nebuchadnezzar, the crown prince of Babylon, made a final defeat of the Assyrian empire, an empire which had been at war with the Medes, the Egyptians and the Babylonians since 626 B.C. This is well-documented in the Nabopolassar Chronicles, which indicates that the Assyrian was in fact "beaten down."

Can it be said then, that the first trumpet blew in 606 B.C., and concerned the area of the Tigris-Euphrates and its relationship to the kingdom of Solomon? Let us continue.

> [8]And the second angel sounded, and as it were a great mountain burning with fire was cast into the sea: and the third part of the sea became blood;
>
> [9]And the third part of the creatures which were in the sea, and had life, died; and the third part of the ships were destroyed.

Our key to the dating of this second trumpet is found in the last sentence fragment – "and the third part of the ships were destroyed." This has meaning if you consider the Battle of Salamis, the naval battle fought between the Greeks and the Persian Empire in September of 480 B.C.

In this battle, the Greeks allowed the Persian navy to sail into the Straits of Salamis, where their large ships bottlenecked one another. The smaller ships of the Greeks were still able to maneuver in the Straits, and were able to sink or capture some 200 Persian ships. This forced Xerxes to retreat back to Asia.

The Battle of Salamis in considered to be the turning point in the course of the conflict between the Greeks and the Persians, and the Greek victory led to the development of western civilization as we know it, making the Battle of Salamis one of the most significant battles in human history.

10And the third angel sounded, and there fell a great star from heaven, burning as it were a lamp, and it fell upon the third part of the rivers, and upon the fountains of waters;

11And the name of the star is called Wormwood: and the third part of the waters became wormwood; and many men died of the waters, because they were made bitter.

This sounding discusses a couple of things, in a literal sense. A "great star from heaven" means in its non-spiritual form an asteroid, meteor or comet. "Burning as it were a lamp" is exactly what one would expect when an asteroid, a meteor or comet (or comet fragment) of some size were to enter the atmosphere on a trajectory of collision with earth. The language that discusses this heavenly body striking "the third part of the rivers, and upon the fountains of waters" gives us several indications that the area hit is that land mass where a third of the rivers of the world are located, i.e., the continent of Asia.

This particular strike poisons the water and many men die. The question is: has this already happened, or is it projected to happen in the future, or both?

Our modern science – a study which has been crippled since the publication of Darwin's "The Origin of Species by means of natural selection; or the preservation of preferred races in the struggle for life" – is just now discovering that the earth may have been hit with 10-megaton violent impacts from comets or asteroids as often as once in every 1,000 years.

The Holocene Impact Working Group claims that evidence for such impacts during the last 10,000 years demonstrates that catastrophic impacts could happen every 1,000 years.[9]

As a consequence, such an impact could have occurred in virtually every epoch. Unfortunately, there is no historical record of such an asteroid strike in Asia, other than the Tunguska Event, a meteor strike in Siberian Russia on June 30, 1908. If such an event occurred, we have not yet found it, and cannot settle its date, although for it to align with the other prophecy in this study, it would necessary have to follow the events of the first and second trumpets in 606 B.C. and 480 B.C. respectively, but before the occurrence of the fourth trumpet, and should necessarily coincide with key battles over the

---

[9] Sandra Blakeslee, Ancient Crash, Epic Wave, New York Times, Science, November 14, 2006.

kingdoms governing the cradle of civilization – the Tigris-Euphrates valley.

While it is not good to speculate, it strikes me that the next most important event in the history of the region is the fall of the Parthian Empire, which occurred on the 28th of April, 224, when Artabanus IV was killed in the battle of Golpayegan by the emerging Persian king named Ardashir. This marker would be consistent with other trumpets in marking significant battles that altered the course of those civilizations that would have great effect on the life of Jerusalem.

The Holocene Impact Working Group has found evidence of a meteoric strike somewhere near the Island of Madagascar in the Indian Ocean that resulted in salt waters overflowing the land with tsunamis as high as

600'. The chevrons evident on the Island give this indication, as does the crater in the Indian Ocean that has been recently discovered at a depth of 12,500 feet.[10] The scientists involved with this study date the crater at around 2,800 B.C., but of course, the inability of scientists to properly date anything without an agenda renders this date useless.

> [12]And the fourth angel sounded, and the third part of the sun was smitten, and the third part of the moon, and the third part of the stars; so as the third part of them was darkened, and the day shone not for a third part of it, and the night likewise.

There are those who date the fourth trumpet as the date of the Battle of Badr on

---

[10] Op. cit.

March 17, 624 A.D. This battle was the turning point in the rise of Islam, as Mohammed defeated the Quraish who outnumbered his forces nearly three to one. The battle is praised in Islamic history as a victory attributable to divine intervention.

As a result of this battle, Islam began to rise, and a third of them (that lived in the region over which these trumpets have dominion) lost the light of the sun (the redemption of Christ) and the third part of the moon (the covenant of Abraham to the old believers) and the third part of the stars (the angels of light). This is of significant spiritual consequence, and is a marker of particularity.

> [13]And I beheld, and heard an angel flying through the midst of heaven, saying with a loud voice, Woe, woe,

woe, to the inhabiters of the earth by reason of the other voices of the trumpet of the three angels, which are yet to sound!

Just to review:

- Announcing the trumpets: The earthquake of Amos 1: 760 B.C.
- First trumpet: Nebuchadnezzar's defeat of the Assyrians in 606 B.C.
- Second trumpet: Greek defeat of the Persian Empire in 480 B.C.
- Third trumpet: Persian defeat of the Parthian Empire in 224 A.D.
- Fourth trumpet: Islamic defeat of the Quraish in 624 A.D.

Let us now consider the timing on the fifth and sixth trumpets.

CHAPTER EIGHT

The sounding of the fifth and sixth trumpets

And the fifth angel sounded, and I saw a star fall from heaven unto the earth: and to him was given the key of the bottomless pit.

And he opened the bottomless pit; and there arose a smoke out of the pit, as the smoke of a great furnace; and the sun and the air were darkened by reason of the smoke of the pit.

And there came out of the smoke locusts upon the earth: and unto them was given power, as the scorpions of the earth have power.

And it was commanded them that they should not hurt the grass of the earth, neither any green thing, neither any tree; but only those men which have not the seal of God in their foreheads.

And to them it was given that they should not kill them, but that they should be tormented five months: and their torment was as the torment of a scorpion, when he striketh a man.

And in those days shall men seek death, and shall not find it; and shall desire to die, and death shall flee from them.

And the shapes of the locusts were like unto horses prepared unto battle; and on their heads were as it were crowns like gold, and their faces were as the faces of men.

And they had hair as the hair of women, and their teeth were as the teeth of lions.

And they had breastplates, as it were breastplates of iron; and the sound of their wings was as the sound of chariots of many horses running to battle.

And they had tails like unto scorpions, and there were stings in their tails: and their power was to hurt men five months.

And they had a king over them, which is the angel of the bottomless pit, whose name in the Hebrew tongue is Abaddon, but in the Greek tongue hath his name Apollyon.

One woe is past; and, behold, there come two woes more hereafter.

-    Revelation 9

Once again we have a reference to "star" falling from heaven. For instance, Isaiah 14:12 gives us the verse: "How you are fallen from heaven, O Day Star, son of Dawn!" (ESV). Most commentators believe that this is a reference to Satan or Lucifer. In fact, the Latin Vulgate interpreted "O Day Star" (a star clustered within a sickle moon), as Lucifer, or light bearer. The rest of the verse gives us a further indication:

> How you are cut down to the ground, you who laid the nations low! You said in your heart, 'I will ascend to heaven; above the stars of God I will set my throne on high; I will sit on the mount of assembly in the far reaches of the north; I will ascend above the heights of the clouds; I will make myself like the Most High.' But you are brought down to Sheol, to the far reaches of the pit.

Jesus gives us a complete affirmation of this account, saying "I saw Satan fall like lightning from heaven." Luke 10:18. Let us therefore conclude that the express meaning of this verse - "And the fifth angel sounded, and I saw a star fall from heaven unto the earth: and to him was given the key of the bottomless pit" - is that Satan fell from heaven to earth following the sounding of the fifth trumpet, and he was given the key to the bottomless pit.

> And he opened the bottomless pit; and there arose a smoke out of the pit, as the smoke of a great furnace; and the sun and the air were darkened by reason of the smoke of the pit.

This passage appears to be a dating consistent with a cataclysmic volcanic eruption, where a "bottomless pit" would open, smoke would arise like the smoke of a great furnace, and the sun and the air would be darkened by reason of the ash of the explosion.

Dr. Kevin Pang of the Jet Propulsion Laboratory has determined that the Kuwae volcano erupted most likely in early 1453, in an eruption that was six times greater than the eruption of Mt. Pinatubo, moving 32-39

cubic kilometers of magma, making the
Kuwae eruption one of the largest in the last
10,000 years. This marks the date of the fifth
trumpet.

> And there came out of the
> smoke locusts upon the earth: and
> unto them was given power, as the
> scorpions of the earth have power.

Out of this smoke come locusts upon
the earth. The "earth" is an interesting
phrase when used in Revelation, particularly
when John references "those who dwell on
the earth", as distinguished from "whose
names are not written in the book of life of
the Lamb". Revelation 13:8. Consider the
Greek interpretation of Amos 7:

> Thus has the Lord God shewed
> me; and, behold, a swarm of locusts
> coming from the east; and, behold, one
> caterpillar, king Gog. And it came to

> pass when he had finished devouring the grass of the land, that I said, Lord God, be merciful; who shall raise up Jacob? for he is small in number. Repent, O Lord, for this. And this shall not be, saith the Lord.
>
> - Amos 7:1-3 (Septuagint)

The book of Amos is a prophecy concerning the coming destruction from the Assyrians on the northern kingdom called Israel. The swarm of locusts coming from the east is most assuredly the Assyrian army whose king – the Assyrian – is Gog. Note also that that the swarm devours the grass.

> And it was commanded them that they should not hurt the grass of the earth, neither any green thing, neither any tree; but only those men which have not the seal of God in their foreheads.

This time, however, the grass of the earth, the green things and the trees will not be harmed. Such an edict is found in the Quran. These "locusts" will also carry a seal of god in their foreheads. Here again, the Quran states that those who are with Muhammad are seen "kneeling and bowing in reverence, seeking his favour and acceptance. Their mark is on their foreheads from the effect of prostrations." Quran 48:29.

> And to them it was given that they should not kill them, but that they should be tormented five months: and their torment was as the torment of a scorpion, when he striketh a man.

Here, the dating of the book of Revelation is once again with us. As I have pointed out, John's reiteration of "time, times and half a time" found in the book of Daniel, lends credence to the same understanding that a day equals a year. From the time the abyss is opened until the torment ends will be five prophetic months. Where a day equals a year, five months is then 150 years (5 months x 30 days). These Islamic warriors would torment men for 150 years.

> And in those days shall men seek death, and shall not find it; and shall desire to die, and death shall flee from them.

There is a period of time when such an event occurred that followed the timing of the four trumpets which precede this event, that is, sometime after 624 A.D. The date is given on the opening of the bottomless pit, which we will see is May 22, 1453. This passage also tells us who these locusts are, because they have over them a certain king, and their allegiance requires that they carry a mark on their forehead.

Although the Islamic world began to unite under the rise of Othman or Osman, the first Caliph over the Islamic Caliphate, who began his sustained campaign against the Greek Byzantine Empire on 1299, conquest of Constantinople was not achieved until May 29, 1453. It is during this battle that the fifth trumpet sounds. The Ottomans then began a sustained war against Christendom to impose the edicts of Islam on Europe. Consider how these Muslim invaders appeared to the defenders of Constantinople in 1453:

> And the shapes of the locusts were like unto horses prepared unto battle; and on their heads were as it were crowns like gold, and their faces were as the faces of men.

Even though this passage appears analogous, consider the descriptions contained therein: "horses prepared unto battle"; "crowns like gold" on their head; with "faces of men." These phrases are totally consistent with Ottoman cavalry wearing their yellow turbans.

> And they had hair as the hair of women, and their teeth were as the teeth of lions.
>
> And they had breastplates, as it were breastplates of iron; and the sound of their wings was as the sound of chariots of many horses running to battle.

We continue our descriptions here, with phrases such as "hair of women" like the long hair of Muslim warriors, "teeth of lions" like grimacing Saracens, wearing "breastplates of iron" and sounding like "chariots of many horses running to battle".

Iron is a significant marker of denotation as well. Consider Surah 57 of the Quran, entitled Iron: "We sent down iron which causes much distress but also has advantages for men, so that God may know who helps Him and His apostles in secret." 57:26.

The passage from the Quran has additional support found in the book of Enoch:

> *And Azâzêl taught men to make swords, and knives, and shields, and breastplates, and made known to them the metals of the earth and the art of working them*, and bracelets, and ornaments, and the use of antimony, and the beautifying of the eyelids, and all kinds of costly stones, and all colouring tinctures. And there arose much godlessness, and they

committed fornication, and they were led astray, and became corrupt in all their ways. Semjâzâ taught enchantments, and root-cuttings, Armârôs the resolving of enchantments, Barâqîjâl, (taught) astrology, Kôkabêl the constellations, Ezêqêêl the knowledge of the clouds, Araqiêl the signs of the earth, Shamsiêl the signs of the sun, and Sariêl the course of the moon. And as men perished, they cried, and their cry went up to heaven . . .

- Enoch 8:1-2

For those who are curious as to who these are, considering the following explanatory chapter from Enoch:

And it came to pass when the children of men had multiplied that in those days were born unto them beautiful and comely daughters. And the angels, the children of the heaven, saw and lusted after them, and said to one another: 'Come, let us choose us wives from among the children of men and beget us children.' And Semjâzâ, who was their leader, said unto them: 'I fear ye will not indeed agree to do this deed, and I alone shall have to pay the penalty of a great sin.' And they all answered him and said: 'Let us all swear an oath, and all bind ourselves by mutual imprecations not to abandon this plan but to do this thing.' Then sware they all together and bound themselves by mutual imprecations upon it. And they were in all two hundred; who descended in the days of Jared on the summit of Mount Hermon, and they called it Mount Hermon, because they had sworn and bound themselves by mutual imprecations upon it. And these are the names of their leaders: Sêmîazâz, their leader, Arâkîba, Râmêêl, Kôkabîêl, Tâmîêl, Râmîêl, Dânêl, Êzêqêêl, Barâqîjâl, Asâêl, Armârôs, Batârêl, Anânêl, Zaqîêl, Samsâpêêl, Satarêl, Tûrêl, Jômjâêl, Sariêl. These are their chiefs of tens.

-Enoch 6:1-8

Let us further consider that these locusts were given the power to hurt men for five months, or 150 years.

> And they had tails like unto scorpions, and there were stings in their tails: and their power was to hurt men five months.

Beginning with the conquest of Constantinople in May of 1453, the locust armies will torment and hurt men until June, 1593. In June, 1593, the power of the Ottoman Empire began its decline, with its defeat in the Battle of Sisak (now modern Croatia). This battle began on June 22, 1593, where 5,000 Christian Croats defended the fortress of Sisak against 12,000 Turks. With the assistance of artillery, the smaller force decimated the Turks, and when the Turks found themselves ambushed between two rivers, they panicked and attempted to flee, resulting in a complete rout. This marked the beginning of the end for the Ottoman Empire.

Our last marker indicating that this reference is to the forces of Islam is given in the following verse:

> And they had a king over them, which is the angel of the bottomless pit, whose name in the Hebrew tongue is Abaddon, but in the Greek tongue hath his name Apollyon.

The king is called Abaddon or Apollyon – both names mean the same: the "destroyer", coincidently one of the 99 beautiful names of Allah found in the Quran.

The fifth trumpet sounded with the eruption of Kuwae during the battle of Constantinople in May, 1453, one of the most famous battles in history.

On May 22, 1453, the moon, symbol of Constantinople, rose in dark eclipse, fulfilling a prophecy on the city's demise. Four days later, the whole city was blotted out by a thick fog, a condition unknown in that part of the world in May, although it is possible that the city was overcome with smoke and ash from the cataclysmic eruption of the Kuwae volcano in the Pacific. On May 25, a thunderstorm burst on the city that was so violent, that it was impossible to stand up against the hail, and the rain came down in such torrents that whole streets were flooded.

On May 26, 1453, the whole city was blotted out by a thick fog, and when the fog lifted that evening, a strange light was seen playing about the dome of the Hagia Sophia, and from the city walls lights were seen in the countryside to the West, far behind the Turkish camp. The light around the dome was interpreted by some as the Holy Spirit departing from the Cathedral, while there was a distant hope that the lights were the campfires of the troops of John Hunyadi who had come to relieve the city.

The conquest of Constantinople was completed on May 29, 1453, and the city was renamed Istanbul in 1930. This conquest was the subject of Islamic prophecy as well: "Constantinople will definitely be conquered one day. What a nice commandment is the commandment that conquers it, what nice soldiers is the soldiers that conquers it."

(*Hadith* of Prophet Muhammad)(source:

Ahmet b. Hanbal, Musned IV, 225.)

> One woe is past; and, behold,
> there come two woes more hereafter.

The fifth woe was completed, and the

sixth trumpet would then sound.

> And the sixth angel sounded,
> and I heard a voice from the four
> horns of the golden altar which is
> before God,

> Saying to the sixth angel which
> had the trumpet, Loose the four angels
> which are bound in the great river
> Euphrates.

Who are these four angels that are

bound in the great river Euphrates? Once

again, we turn to the book of Enoch for

answers:

And the Lord said unto Michael: 'Go, **bind** Semjâzâ and his associates who have united themselves with women so as to have defiled themselves with them in all their uncleanness. And when their sons have slain one another, and they have seen the destruction of their beloved ones, bind them fast for seventy generations in the **valleys** of the earth, till the day of their judgment and of their consummation, till the judgment that is forever and ever is consummated.

- Enoch 10:11-12

Enoch tells us why the angels are bound, and tells us who those angels are that are bound. There are other references to these angels who are bound in this area of the world. For instance, the heavenly being that confronts Daniel in his Chapter 10 is withstood by twenty-four days by "the prince of the King of Persia" and is eventually helped by the angel Michael. Daniel 10:13. The withstanding of a heavenly being can only be through another heavenly being – one bound within Persia.

The four angels bound in the great river Euphrates are similar in reference to the four angels of the four winds, as described in the Olivet sermon found in Matthew 24:

> Immediately after the tribulation of those days shall the sun be darkened, and the moon shall not give her light, and the stars shall fall from heaven, and the powers of the heavens shall be shaken:

> And then shall appear the sign of the Son of man in heaven: and then shall all the tribes of the earth mourn, and they shall see the Son of man coming in the clouds of heaven with power and great glory.

And he shall send his angels
with a great sound of a trumpet, and
they shall gather together his elect
from the four winds, from one end of
heaven to the other.

The angles who gather the elect gather from "the four winds" which is defined as "from one end of heaven to the other". The four angels bound in the great river Euphrates, given a similar interpretation, would mean all those who are prepared to slay men from within all points of the kingdom that governs the Euphrates.

And the four angels were
loosed, which were prepared for an
hour, and a day, and a month, and a
year, for to slay the third part of men.

As we once again consider that a day equals a year, an hour ($1/24^{th}$ of a day), a day, a month and a year amounts to 396 days and

1/24th of a day. When a day equals a year for purposes of unsealing prophecy, we have 396 years and 15 days (half a month/1/24th of a year).

> And the number of the army of the horsemen were two hundred thousand thousand: and I heard the number of them.

> And thus I saw the horses in the vision, and them that sat on them, having breastplates of fire, and of jacinth, and brimstone: and the heads of the horses were as the heads of lions; and out of their mouths issued fire and smoke and brimstone.

> By these three was the third part of men killed, by the fire, and by the smoke, and by the brimstone, which issued out of their mouths.

> For their power is in their mouth, and in their tails: for their tails were like unto serpents, and had heads, and with them they do hurt.

And the rest of the men which were not killed by these plagues yet repented not of the works of their hands, that they should not worship devils, and idols of gold, and silver, and brass, and stone, and of wood: which neither can see, nor hear, nor walk:

Neither repented they of their murders, nor of their sorceries, nor of their fornication, nor of their thefts.

Let us then calculate the timing of the sixth trumpet. The fifth trumpet sounds with the eruption of Kuwae in May, 1453. The Ottoman horsemen then torment men for 150 years, until their ascendency is arrested at the battle of Sisek in June 22, 1593. The four angels bound at the Euphrates are then loosed to prepare for the sounding of the sixth trumpet, which is to occur 396 years and 15 days later, or July 8, 1989.

To properly calculate this date, however, it is necessary to add to it one hour, one day, one month and one year. July 8, 1989 takes us to August 9, 1990, the date that George H. W. Bush decided to launch Operation Desert Storm against the nation of Iraq as a result of its invasion of Kuwait on August 2, 1990.

This event – the rise of the Coalition Forces against the land of Babylon, was also foretold in a three-part prophecy found in Isaiah 13:

> The burden of Babylon, which Isaiah the son of Amoz did see.
>
> Lift ye up a banner upon the high mountain, exalt the voice unto them, shake the hand, that they may go into the gates of the nobles.
>
> I have commanded my sanctified ones, I have also called **my mighty ones for mine anger**, even **them that rejoice in my highness**.
>
> The noise of a multitude in the mountains, like as of a great people; a tumultuous noise of **the kingdoms of nations gathered together**: the LORD of hosts mustereth the host of the battle.
>
> **They come from a far country**, from the end of heaven, even the LORD, and

the weapons of his indignation, to destroy the whole land.

-   Isaiah 13:1-5

This particular scripture seems to be fairly explicit. The kingdoms of nations – the coalition forces – gathered together, coming from a far country, using weapons of indignation. Consider also that even after the destruction of the armed forces of Iraq, Saddam Hussein "neither repented they of their murders, nor of their sorceries, nor of their fornication, nor of their thefts." As a consequence, Iraq was invaded once again, Baghdad taken, Saddam Hussein executed, and the power structure completely overthrown.

> [13]And I beheld, and heard an angel flying through the midst of heaven, saying with a loud voice, Woe, woe,

woe, to the inhabiters of the earth by reason of the other voices of the trumpet of the three angels, which are yet to sound!

Just to review:

- Announcing the trumpets: The earthquake of Amos 1: 760 B.C.
- First trumpet: Nebuchadnezzar's defeat of the Assyrians in 606 B.C.
- Second trumpet: Greek defeat of the Persian Empire in 480 B.C.
- Third trumpet: Persian defeat of the Parthian Empire in 224 A.D.
- Fourth trumpet: Islamic defeat of the Quraish in 624 A.D.
- Fifth trumpet: Ottoman defeat of the Byzantine Empire in 1453 A.D.
- Sixth trumpet: US Coalition assault on Iraq in 1990 A.D.

Then I saw another mighty angel coming down from heaven, wrapped in a cloud, with a rainbow over his head, and his face was like the sun, and his legs like pillars of fire. He had a little scroll open in his hand. And he set his right foot on the sea, and his left foot on the land, and called out with a loud voice, like a lion roaring. When he called out, the seven thunders sounded. And when the seven thunders had sounded, I was about to write, but I heard a voice from heaven saying, "Seal up what the seven thunders have said, and do not write it down." And the angel whom I saw standing on the sea and on the land raised his right hand to heaven and swore by him who lives forever and ever, who created heaven and what is in it, the earth and what is in it, and the sea and what is in it, that **there would be no more delay, but that in the days of the trumpet call to be sounded by the seventh angel, the mystery of God would be fulfilled, just as he announced to his servants the prophets**.

-    Revelation 10:1-7

CHAPTER NINE

The Second Realization of
Daniel's Seventy Weeks

Of course, since then, there has been
another command to rebuild Jerusalem,
issued by the United Nations on November
30, 1947 (UN Resolution #181. See
Addendum A.

> Independent Arab and Jewish States
> and the Special International Regime
> for **the City of Jerusalem**, set forth in
> Part III of this Plan, **shall come into
> existence in Palestine two months
> after the evacuation of the armed
> forces of the mandatory Power has
> been completed but in any case not
> later than 1 October 1948**. The
> boundaries of the Arab State, the
> Jewish State, and the City of Jerusalem
> shall be as described in Parts II and III
> below. United Nations General
> Assembly Resolution 181, November

29, 1947, PLAN OF PARTITION WITH ECONOMIC UNION, Part I. - Future Constitution and Government of Palestine, A. TERMINATION OF MANDATE, PARTITION AND INDEPENDENCE.

Let us now consider the prophecy anew, and in the second interpretation of the term Shabuwa, which means both a period of seven days, and also the feast of weeks (Shavuot or Pentacost). We have looked at the realization of this prophecy as a period of seven days. However, the prophecy gives another revelation when it is considered as seventy Shavuots, or seventy literal years. In our latter days, this prophecy therefore begins on the date of the United Nations General Assembly Resolution 181, November 29, 1947.

Seventy weeks [70 years in this understanding] are determined upon thy people and upon thy holy city, to finish the transgression, and to make an end of sins, and to make reconciliation for iniquity, and to bring in everlasting righteousness, and to seal up the vision and prophecy, and to anoint the most Holy.

Know therefore and understand, that from the going forth of the commandment to restore and to build Jerusalem [1947] unto the Messiah the Prince shall be seven weeks [7 years], and threescore and two weeks [62 years]: the street shall be built again, and the wall, even in troublous times [Jerusalem rebuilt following the creation of the Israeli nation].

And after threescore and two weeks shall Messiah be cut off [62 weeks], but not for himself: and the people of the prince that shall come [the forces of Ezekiel 38] shall destroy the city and the sanctuary[2009]; and the end thereof shall be with a flood, and unto the end of the war [7 years] desolations are determined.

And he shall confirm the covenant with many for one week [7 years]: and in the midst of the week [3 ½ years] he shall cause the sacrifice and the oblation [worship] to cease, and for the overspreading of abominations he shall make it desolate, even until the consummation [the end of the 69th week], and that determined shall be poured upon the desolate.

In the seventieth week, God will finish the transgression, make an end of sins, make reconciliation for iniquity, and will bring in everlasting righteousness, which will seal up the vision and prophecy, and which will anoint the most Holy, which is to say that this prophecy will be realized with the second coming of Christ.

The Olivet Prophecy of Luke 21

This prophecy is in the process of being fulfilled as we speak. Consider the words of Jesus, in Luke 21:

> And he said, Take heed that ye be not deceived: for many shall come in my name, saying, I am Christ; and the time draweth near: go ye not therefore after them.

> But when ye shall hear of wars and commotions, be not terrified: for these things must first come to pass; but the end is not by and by.

> Then said he unto them, Nation shall rise against nation, and kingdom against kingdom:

> And great earthquakes shall be in divers places, and famines, and pestilences; and fearful sights and great signs shall there be from heaven.

> But before all these, they shall lay their hands on you, and persecute

you, delivering you up to the synagogues, and into prisons, being brought before kings and rulers for my name's sake.

And it shall turn to you for a testimony.

Settle it therefore in your hearts, not to meditate before what ye shall answer:

For I will give you a mouth and wisdom, which all your adversaries shall not be able to gainsay nor resist.

And ye shall be betrayed both by parents, and brethren, and kinsfolks, and friends; and some of you shall they cause to be put to death.

And ye shall be hated of all men for my name's sake.

But there shall not an hair of your head perish.

In your patience possess ye
your souls.

And when ye shall see
Jerusalem compassed with armies,
then know that the desolation thereof
is nigh.

Then let them which are in
Judaea flee to the mountains; and let
them which are in the midst of it
depart out; and let not them that are
in the countries enter thereinto.

For these be the days of
vengeance, that all things which are
written may be fulfilled.

But woe unto them that are
with child, and to them that give suck,
in those days! for there shall be great
distress in the land, and wrath upon
this people.

And they shall fall by the edge
of the sword, and shall be led away
captive into all nations: and Jerusalem
shall be trodden down of the Gentiles,

until the times of the Gentiles be fulfilled.

And there shall be signs in the sun, and in the moon, and in the stars; and upon the earth distress of nations, with perplexity; the sea and the waves roaring;

Men's hearts failing them for fear, and for looking after those things which are coming on the earth: for the powers of heaven shall be shaken.

And then shall they see the Son of man coming in a cloud with power and great glory.

And when these things begin to come to pass, then look up, and lift up your heads; for your redemption draweth nigh. Luke 21:8-28

The Parable of the Fig Tree

And he spake to them a parable; Behold the fig tree, and all the trees; When they now shoot forth, ye see and know of your own selves that summer is now nigh at hand.

So likewise ye, when ye see these things come to pass, know ye that the kingdom of God is nigh at hand. Verily I say unto you, This generation shall not pass away, till all be fulfilled. Heaven and earth shall pass away: but my words shall not pass away.

And take heed to yourselves, lest at any time your hearts be overcharged with surfeiting, and drunkenness, and cares of this life, and so that day come upon you unawares.

For as a snare shall it come on all them that dwell on the face of the whole earth.

Watch ye therefore, and pray always, that ye may be accounted worthy to escape all these things that shall come to pass, and to stand before the Son of man.

One meaning of a full generation is the period of 70 years as described in Psalms 90:10. The beginning of the last full generation before the return of the Messiah to Jerusalem, therefore, may be marked by the birth of the modern Jewish state in May 1948. Jesus proclaims that "this generation shall not pass away, till all be fulfilled." This prophecy in its second realization should therefore be completed in its entirety before 2018.

The Olivet Analysis

Let's take the Olivet sermon, as this passage in Luke 21 is known, passage by passage and see if it is being realized.

False Christs

> And he said, Take heed that ye be not deceived: for many shall come in my name, saying, I am Christ; and the time draweth near: go ye not therefore after them.

It seems like we have one false Christ after another. Currently, we are dealing with Jose Luis de Jesus Miranda, who claims his is Jesus Christ Man and the second coming of Christ. He owns three Rolex watches. There is another false Christ, however, that is the subject of this book. You will notice that Jesus does not say that many will be deceived by the "Antichrist" – he says that people will be deceived by someone *claiming* to be Christ, saying "I am Christ."

Wars and Commotions

Next, Jesus discusses that which engenders fear and usually triggers prophetic inclination: war.

> But when ye shall hear of wars and commotions, be not terrified: for these things must first come to pass; but the end is not by and by.

Just because we have wars does not mean that we have reached the end of days. Wars and commotions, even world wars, are not an indicator of the coming of the Kingdom of God. Jesus goes on to spell out what we would see when we are reaching those days

> Then said he unto them, Nation shall rise against nation, and kingdom against kingdom:

This prophecy predicts both war and revolution – civil wars – as nations rise against nations and kingdoms rise against kingdoms. If this is an inclusive prophecy, no nation on earth will be free of being at war and in civil war at the same time. Civil war is present in Southeast Asia, and throughout Africa. Civil strife is present in China, India, Russia, Greece, Spain, Italy, Denmark, France, the UK, New Zealand, Korea, Kenya, Congo, Nigeria, Sudan, Somalia, Morocco, Algeria, Iran, Iraq, Turkey, Armenia, Azerbaijan, Mongolia, Columbia, Peru, Bolivia, and is now appearing in Canada. It may yet emerge in the US as well. We are nearing this mark on every continent on earth even as we speak. If this is an inclusive prophecy, complete international chaos is just around the corner as nation-states, having forfeited the rule of law in favor of raw power find themselves with neither. It seems that the war

prophesized here is total worldwide war –
World War III. Is this now possible?

The rise of irrational post-modernism
now leaves governments in an interesting
quandary: how can they claim a legitimate
right to govern, when the governed do not
accept reasonable arguments as grounds for
consent? A robust barbarianism is upon us
all now at a worldwide level, which has no
resting point other than death. The rebels in
Sri Lanka, or in Myanmar, or in Kenya, or in
the Congo, or in Greece, or in Chechnya, or in
Mongolia, have no rationale that they
espouse. There is no Marxist idealism, or
Rousseauian virtue – there is only a quest for
power and a willingness to kill to obtain it.
This is a cocktail that has been mixed by the
world powers over the last 62 years, and the
blend is now ready for consumption.

Earthquakes

And great earthquakes shall be In divers places, and famines, and pestilences; and fearful sights and great signs shall there be from heaven.

This prophecy too is being realized. Here's this year's roster of significant earthquakes, including the quake in Haiti, that took the largest number of lives ever lost in a natural disaster:

Earthquakes

- Magnitude 5.8 PUERTO RICO May 16, 2010
- Magnitude 7.2 NORTHERN SUMATRA, INDONESIA May 09, 2010
- Magnitude 6.5 SOUTHEAST OF TAIWAN April 26, 2010
- Magnitude 4.9 UTAH April 15, 2010
- Magnitude 6.9 SOUTHERN QINGHAI, CHINA April 13, 2010
- Magnitude 6.3 SPAIN April 11, 2010

- Magnitude 6.8 SOLOMON ISLANDS April 11, 2010
- Magnitude 7.8 NORTHERN SUMATRA, INDONESIA April 06, 2010
- Magnitude 7.2 BAJA CALIFORNIA, MEXICO April 04, 2010
- Magnitude 4.4 GREATER LOS ANGELES AREA, CALIFORNIA March 16, 2010
- Magnitude 6.7 OFFSHORE BIO-BIO, CHILE March 16, 2010
- Magnitude 6.5 NEAR THE EAST COAST OF HONSHU, JAPAN March 14, 2010
- Magnitude 6.9 LIBERTADOR O HIGGINS, CHILE March 11, 2010
- Magnitude 6.1 EASTERN TURKEY March 08, 2010
- Magnitude 6.8 SOUTHERN SUMATRA, INDONESIA March 05, 2010
- Magnitude 6.6 OFFSHORE BIO-BIO, CHILE March 05, 2010
- Magnitude 8.8 OFFSHORE MAULE, CHILE February 27, 2010
- Magnitude 7.0 RYUKYU ISLANDS, JAPAN February 26, 2010

- Magnitude 6.9 CHINA-RUSSIA-NORTH KOREA BORDER REGION February 18, 2010
- Magnitude 3.8 ILLINOIS February 10, 2010
- Magnitude 5.9 OFFSHORE NORTHERN CALIFORNIA February 04, 2010
- Magnitude 6.2 BOUGAINVILLE REGION, PAPUA NEW GUINEA February 01, 2010
- Magnitude 5.9 HAITI REGION January 20, 2010
- Magnitude 4.0 OKLAHOMA January 15, 2010
- Magnitude 7.0 HAITI REGION January 12, 2010
- Magnitude 6.5 OFFSHORE NORTHERN CALIFORNIA January 10, 2010
- Magnitude 4.1 SAN FRANCISCO BAY AREA, CALIFORNIA January 07, 2010
- Magnitude 6.8 SOLOMON ISLANDS January 05, 2010
- Magnitude 7.1 SOLOMON ISLANDS January 03, 2010
- Magnitude 6.6 SOLOMON ISLANDS January 03, 2010

Recent Yellowstone Earthquakes Are Centered Under the Ancient Yellowstone Supervolcano's Caldera

It is not unusual for there to be small earthquakes in the Yellowstone Park area, however the recent spate of Yellowstone earthquakes are different. The University of Utah publishes a map of recent Yellowstone earthquakes online. The map showed 146 earthquakes in the Yellowstone National Park area from December 28, 2008 and January 2, 2009, most of which occurred underneath the ancient Yellowstone volcano. Many of these quakes registered over 3.0 on the Richter scale and the strongest reaching a 3.9 reading.

Since then, the 2010 records have increased considerably. The University of Utah Seismograph Stations reports that a period of increased seismic activity began on January 17, 2010 and multiplied into a swarm of earthquakes. The largest earthquake in the swarm as of 7 AM MST, February 03, 2010, has been a magnitude 3.8. There have been 1,719 located earthquakes in the swarm of magnitude 0.3 to 3.8. This includes 14 events of magnitude larger than 3, with 135 events of magnitude 2 to 3, and 1,570 events of magnitude less than 2. There have been multiple personal reports of ground shaking from observers inside the Park and in surrounding areas for some of the larger events.[11]

For reference, an earthquake with a strength of 4.0 is capable of causing moderate

---

[11]

http://www.seis.utah.edu/EQCENTER/PRESS/yell_press.htm

damage.

Yellowstone National Park is the home of the Old Faithful Geyser which derives its heat from a shallow, five to ten mile deep pool of magma that lies below Yellowstone. The Yellowstone caldera is, in fact, the remnants of a very large volcanic event that occurred hundreds of thousands of years ago. The area is still very geologically active and, according to the University of Utah's earthquake center, is the site of 1000-2000 small earthquakes every year, but they say, this recent activity is much higher than average.

The Yellowstone Supervolcano is Largest Volcano in the US. With all the shaking going on in Yellowstone Park, it might be worth the time to consider the possible effects if the supervolcano under the park were to erupt again. The last time the Yellowstone supervolcano erupted was approximately 6,400 years ago, says Larry Hanlon in his article "America's Explosive Park" on the Discover Channel website. He also notes that the last time the Yellowstone volcano erupted, it was about *8000 times more destructive than the Mount St. Helens* eruption. It has, he says, the potential to be even more powerful than that. If these Yellowstone earthquakes are a precursor to another eruption, the damage would almost certainly be more catastrophic than we can imagine. Aside from the destruction force of the explosion, the tremendous amounts of ash that would be released into the atmosphere would certainly have a dramatic, if temporary, effect on the Earth's climate. It is possible that the ash would block enough sunlight globally to cause a year or two of the coldest weather on record. Not to mention that the Eastern half of the United States would likely be covered in abrasive volcanic ash as it fell from the sky.

It is not certain if these recent Yellowstone earthquakes are the result of existing, but undiscovered fault lines in the area, or if they are related to increased geothermal activity of the Yellowstone volcano. While the possibility of a major eruption at Yellowstone remains extremely unlikely, the volatility of the area reminds us how marvelous and fragile some of our country's natural wonders can be. Even without a major eruption, places like Old Faithful could be disrupted by a minor shift in the geothermal conditions at Yellowstone, just as natural aging and the forces of the weather caused the collapse of the Wall Arch earlier this year at Arches National Park in Utah.[12]

Now consider the prophecy of the sixth seal set forth in Revelation 6:

> I looked when He opened the sixth seal, and behold, there was a great earthquake; and the sun became black as sackcloth of hair, and the moon became like blood. And the stars of heaven fell to the earth, as a fig tree drops its late figs when it is shaken by a mighty wind. Then the sky receded as a scroll when it is rolled up, and every mountain and

---

[12] Do Yellowstone Earthquakes Foretell Yellowstone Volcano Eruption? Brad Sylvester, Associated Content, December 30, 2008.
http://www.associatedcontent.com/article/1348555/do_yellowstone_earthquakes_foretell.html?page=2&cat=8

island was moved out of its place. And the kings of the earth, the great men, the rich men, the commanders, the mighty men, every slave and every free man, hid themselves in the caves and in the rocks of the mountains, and said to the mountains and rocks, "Fall on us and hide us from the face of Him who sits on the throne and from the wrath of the Lamb! For the great day of His wrath has come, and who is able to stand?" Revelation 6:12-16.

This prophecy sure seems to speak of the kind of Yellowstone Volcano eruption as described in the AC article. "I looked when He opened the sixth seal, and behold, there was a great earthquake; and the sun became black as sackcloth of hair, and the moon became like blood." Brad Sylvester gives us an indication that there would be a tremendous "destruction force of the explosion," and that there would be "tremendous amounts of ash that would be released into the atmosphere." How much ash if the explosion was 8,000 times as powerful as Mount St. Helens?

Sylvester claims that such ash "would certainly have a dramatic, if temporary, effect on the Earth's climate." "We might *expect the ash to block enough sunlight globally to cause a year or two of the coldest weather on record.*" The sun would become black as sackcloth of hair, and the moon would become like blood. Such an explosion would most assuredly be accompanied with a great earthquake – maybe the greatest earthquake the world has ever seen.

However, it now appears that Yellowstone may not be the only culprit. The recent eruption of Iceland's Eyjafjallajokull has disrupted air traffic across Europe for several weeks. Now geologists are saying that the volcano could carry on for many months — and possibly years.

These same geologists have also warned of a serious threat from a fourth volcano, Katla, which lies 15 miles to the east of Eyjafjallajokull. Two of its past three eruptions seemed to be triggered by those of its smaller neighbour and a report issued just before Eyjafjallajokull blew suggested Katla was "close to failure [eruption]".

In case that is not enough, there are three other volcanoes cited by Thordarson as being potentially close to a large eruption, namely, Grimsvotn, Hekla and Askja — all of which are bigger than Eyjafjallajokull.

In the past, these eruptions have proved to be devastating. Hekla alone has erupted about 20 times since AD874, pouring out a total of two cubic miles of lava from a line of fissures that stretches 3 miles across the mountain.

There was a minor eruption in 2000 and geologists have reported that snow is once again melting on Hekla's summit, suggesting that magma is rising.

Grimsvotn, another highly active volcano, lies under the huge Vatnajokull glacier in Iceland's southeast. An eruption in 1996 saw much of this glacial ice melt, causing a flood that washed away the country's main ring road.

It is linked to the massive Laki fissure volcano whose 1783 eruption ejected so much ash into the atmosphere that it cooled the entire northern hemisphere for nearly three years. The resulting low temperatures caused crop failures and famines that killed 2 million people and helped trigger the French Revolution.[13]

Famines

Widespread earthquakes (*not* earthquakes of increasing severity) are not all that is predicted in this prophecy. There is also famine. Consider the following story out of United Kingdom's *The Guardian,*[14]

---

[13] Jonathan Leake and Chris Hastings, Times Online, May 16, 2010
Scientists forecast decades of ash clouds, *Many more of Iceland's volcanoes seem to be stirring,*.
http://www.timesonline.co.uk/tol/news/uk/article7127706.ece

[14] http://www.guardian.co.uk/world/2008/mar/23/india:

*One million face famine after
rats feast on crops*

The people of Mizoram, a tiny,
remote state of north-east India
squeezed between Burma and
Bangladesh, have known for the past
48 years that they would face famine
in 2008. Confirmation came last
November when the local species of
bamboo that dominates the state's
landscape began to burst into flower -
a peculiar ecological phenomenon that
happens about twice a century.
A plague of rats rapidly
followed, feasting on the bamboo's
protein-rich avocado-like fruit, before
swarming to consume the farmers'
rice paddies, grain harvests and food
stockpiles. Now up to a million people
are facing hunger, according to aid
agencies.

The United Nations has weighed in as
the entity has sought to maintain nutrition

levels worldwide. In an article of February 2006 the following statement was made:

> The United Nations warned yesterday that it no longer has enough money to keep global malnutrition at bay this year in the face of a dramatic upward surge in world commodity prices, which have created a "new face of hunger".
>
> "We will have a problem in coming months," said Josette Sheeran, the head of the UN's World Food Programme (WFP). "We will have a significant gap if commodity prices remain this high, and we will need an extra half billion dollars just to meet existing assessed needs."
>
> With voluntary contributions from the world's wealthy nations, the WFP feeds 73 million people in 78 countries, less than a 10th of the total number of the world's undernourished. Its agreed budget for 2008 was $2.9bn (£1.5bn). But with annual food price increases around the world of up to 40% and dramatic hikes in fuel costs, that budget is no

longer enough even to maintain current food deliveries.

The numbers appear to be rather large. According to Bread for the World, the world is facing a hunger crisis unlike anything it has seen in more than 50 years. 1.02 billion people are hungry. Every day, almost 16,000 children die from hunger-related causes. That's one child every five seconds. An additional 100 million people in 70 developing countries have fallen into poverty because of a spike in food prices, pushing the total number of people in extreme poverty to more than 1.4 billion.[15]

Let us consider for a moment that the United Nations estimates that there are approximately 750 million people who are

---

[15] http://www.bread.org/hunger/global/

undernourished. Let us also consider that this reference was made before the worldwide financial collapse of the fall of 2008. In short, this crisis is just beginning.

Great Signs from Heaven

We begin not with the sign of a comet, although there are interesting facts concerning a collision by a comet with Jupiter. Instead, we begin with the sun's activity over recent years.

Solar flares

On October 28, 2008, our Sun produced one of the most powerful solar flares in recorded history. Seen across the electromagnetic spectrum, the Sun briefly became over 100 times brighter in X-rays than normal. Over the next few days, as energetic particles emitted from these regions strike the Earth, satellite communications might be affected and auroras might develop. The flare and resulting CME, emitted from giant sunspot group 10486, was captured above as it happened by the by the LASCO Instrument aboard the Sun-orbiting SOHO satellite. The disk of the Sun is covered to accentuate surrounding areas. The time-lapse movie shows the tremendous explosion in frames separated in real time by about 30 minutes each. The frames appear progressively noisier as protons from the flare begin to strike the detector. The SOHO satellite has been put in a temporary safe mode to avoid damage from the solar particle storm.[16]

No Solar Activity

I'm writing this after doing an exhaustive search to see what sort of solar activity has occurred lately, and I find there is little to report. With the exception of the briefly increased

---

[16] A Powerful Solar Flare, NASA, Robert Namiroff & Jay Bonnell, October 29, 2003.
http://apod.nasa.gov/apod/ap031029.html

solar wind from a coronal hole, there is almost no significant solar activity.

The sun has gone quiet. Really quiet.

It is normal for our sun to have quiet periods between solar cycles, but we've seen months and months of next to nothing, and the start of Solar cycle 24 seems to have materialized then abruptly disappeared. The reverse polarity sunspot that signaled the start of cycle 24 on January 4th, dissolved within two days after that.

Of course we've known that the sunspot cycle has gone low, which is also to be expected for this period of the cycle. Note that NOAA still has two undecided scenarios for cycle 24 Lower than normal, or higher than normal, as indicated on the graph below:

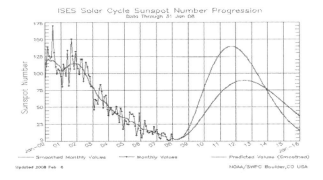

But the real news is just how quiet the sun's magnetic field has been in the past couple of years. From the data provided by NOAA's Space Weather Prediction Center (SWPC) you can see just how little magnetic field activity there has been. I've graphed it below:

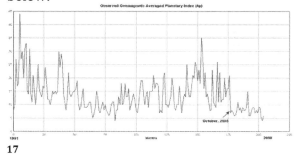

17

---

[17] Where have all the sunspots gone? What's Up With That? Anthony Watts, February 13, 2008.

Blood Moons

A Christian pastor who teaches the Old Testament roots of Christianity has proposed that a rare string of lunar and solar eclipses that are projected to fall on Passover seven years from now could signal the "Second Coming" of Jesus Christ.

"God wants us to look at the biblical calendar," says Mark Biltz, pastor of El Shaddai Ministries in Bonney Lake, Wash. "The reason we need to be watching is [because] He will signal His appearance. But we have to know what to be watching as well. So we need to be watching the biblical holidays."

Biltz said he's been studying prophecies that focus on the sun and moon,

http://wattsupwiththat.com/2008/02/13/where-have-all-the-sunspots-gone/

even going back to the book of Genesis where it states the lights in the sky would be "be for signs, and for seasons."

"It means a signal, kind of like 'one if by land, two if by sea.' It's like God wants to signal us," he said. "The Hebrew word implies ... not only is it a signal, but it's a signal for coming or His appearing."

Biltz adds the word "seasons" implies appointed times for God's feasts and festivals.

"When we hear the word feast, we think food. But the Hebrew word has nothing to do with food. It has to do with a divine appointment, as if God has a day timer, and He says, 'OK, I'm gonna' mark the day and the time when I'm going to signal My appearance.'"

In the Old Testament, the prophet Joel states, "The sun shall be turned into darkness, and the moon into blood, before the great and the terrible day of the LORD come." (Joel 2:31)

In the New Testament, Jesus is quoted as saying, "Immediately after the tribulation of those days shall the sun be darkened, and the moon shall not give her light ... And then shall appear the sign of the Son of man in heaven: and then shall all the tribes of the earth mourn, and they shall see the Son of man coming in the clouds of heaven with power and great glory." (Matthew 24:29-30)

Thus, Biltz began focusing on the precise times of both solar and lunar eclipses, sometimes called "blood moons" since the moon often takes on a bloody color. He logged onto NASA's eclipse website which provides precision tracking of the celestial events.

He noted a rare phenomenon of four consecutive total lunar eclipses, known as a tetrad. He says during this century, tetrads occur at least six times, but what's interesting is that the only string of four consecutive blood moons that coincide with Passover in the spring and the autumn's Feast of Tabernacles (also called Succoth) occurs between 2014 and 2015 on today's Gregorian calendar.

"The fact that it doesn't happen again in this century I think is very significant," Biltz explains. "So then I looked at last century, and, believe it or not, the last time that four blood red moons occurred together was in 1967 and 1968 tied to Jerusalem recaptured by Israel."

He then started to notice a pattern of the tetrads.

"What's significant to me is that even before 1967 the next time that you had four blood red moons again was right after Israel became a nation in '48, it happened again in 1949 and 1950 ... on Passover and Succoth. You didn't have any astronomical tetrads in the 1800s, the 1700s, the 1600s. In the 1500s, there were six, but none of those fell on Passover and Succoth."

When checking the schedule for solar eclipses, Biltz found two – one on the first day of the Hebrew year and the next on the high holy day of Rosh Hashanah, the first day of the seventh Hebrew month. Both of these take place in the 2014-2015 year.[18]

---

[18] Blood Moon Eclipses: 2nd Coming in 2015? Unleavened Bread Ministries, Joe Kovacs, April 30, 2008.
http://www.unleavenedbreadministries.org/?page=bloodmoon

Here's another sign in the heavens for you, seen on March 21, 2008, this time according to NASA:

Astronomers are familiar with seeing amazing things through their telescopes. But nothing prepared them for an incredible explosion detected early Wednesday morning by NASA's Swift satellite. At 2:12 a.m. EDT, Swift detected an explosion from deep space that was so powerful that its afterglow was briefly visible to the naked eye. Even more astonishing, the explosion itself took place halfway across the visible universe!

Never before has anything so far away come even close to naked-eye visibility. The explosion was so far away that it took its light

7,500,000,000 (7.5 billion) years to reach Earth! In fact, the explosion took place so long ago that Earth had not yet come into existence.

"No other known object or type of explosion could be seen by the naked eye at such an immense distance," says Swift science team member Stephen Holland of NASA's Goddard Space Flight Center in Greenbelt, Md. "We don't know yet if anyone was looking at the afterglow at the time it brightened to peak visibility. But if someone just happened to be looking at the right place at the right time, they saw the most distant object ever seen by human eyes without optical aid."[19]

Christian Persecution

But before all these, they shall lay their hands on you, and persecute you, delivering you up to the synagogues, and into prisons, being brought before kings and rulers for my name's sake.

Here is an interesting prophecy in Luke 21, because it specifies a certain timing: "*before* all these (earthquakes, volcanic eruptions with ash covering the earth, blocking the sun, and the blood red moon eclipses), they shall lay their hands on you, and persecute you . . ."

---

[19] A Stellar Explosion You Could See on Earth! March 21, 2008, NASA
http://www.nasa.gov/mission_pages/swift/bursts/brightest_grb.html

The prediction of the great earthquake is the sixth seal in Revelation. Let us see if persecution precedes such a seal:

> When He opened the fifth seal, I saw under the altar the souls of those who had been slain for the word of God and for the testimony which they held. And they cried with a loud voice, saying, "How long, O Lord, holy and true, until You judge and avenge our blood on those who dwell on the earth?" Then a white robe was given to each of them; and it was said to them that they should rest a little while longer, until both *the number of* their fellow servants and their brethren, who would be killed as they *were,* was completed. Revelation 6:9-11.

Canadian Human Rights Commission

Consider the actions of the Canadian Human Rights Commission, one of the top persecutorial institutions in the world when it comes to punishing Christians in the public square.

The Canadian Human Rights Commission administers the Canadian Human Rights Act and is responsible for ensuring compliance with the Canadian Employment Equity Act. Both laws ensure that the principles of equal opportunity and non-discrimination are followed in all areas of Canadian federal jurisdiction.

Part I, section 13 provides as follows:

(1) It is a discriminatory practice for a person or a group of persons acting in concert to communicate telephonically or to cause to be so communicated, repeatedly, in whole or in part by means of the facilities of a telecommunication undertaking within the legislative authority of Parliament, any matter that is likely to expose a person or persons to hatred

or contempt by reason of the fact that that person or those persons are identifiable on the basis of a prohibited ground of discrimination.

Prohibited grounds of discrimination are set forth in Part I, paragraph 1, to wit: "(1) For all purposes of this Act, the prohibited grounds of discrimination are race, national or ethnic origin, colour, religion, age, sex, sexual orientation, marital status, family status, disability and conviction for which a pardon has been granted."

Canadian Richard Warman, a former Human Rights Commission employee has used this act for a continuous income stream, targeting Christians and Jews for persecution in front of the HRC tribunals.

To date, Richard Warman has filed 26 complaints against named respondents with the *Canadian Human Rights Commission.*

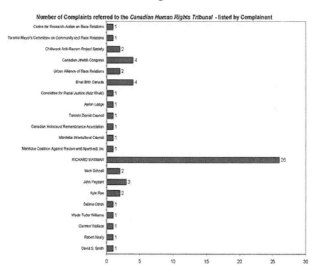

Number of Complaints referred to the *Canadian Human Rights Tribunal* - listed by Complainant

Warman has brought actions under Section 13 against Melissa Guille, Canadian Heritage Alliance, Alexan Kulbashian, Affordable Web Space, James Richardson, Marc Lemire, Glenn Bahr, Western Canada for Us, Ciaran Paul Donnelly, Jessica

Beaumont, Terry Tremaine, Peter Kouba, Craig Harrison, Bobby Wilkinson, Alexandro Di Civita, Elizabeth Lampman, World Church of the Creator, Fred Kyburz, Tomasz Winnicki, Eldon Warman, Jason Ouwendyk and Northern Alliance.

Many actions have been brought against members of the Christian community for referring to Leviticus 20 or Romans 1 which declares homosexuality to be a sin. That, in the eyes of Richard Warman, is sufficient to warrant prosecution under the Canadian Human Rights Act.

Organ Harvesting in China

It is alleged that there are victims of live organ harvesting throughout China. The allegation is that organ harvesting is inflicted on unwilling Falun Gong practitioners, Tibetans, Christians, Uighurs, democracy activists and human rights defenders, at a wide variety of locations, pursuant to a systematic policy, in large numbers.

Organ harvesting is a step in organ transplants. The purpose of organ harvesting is to provide organs for transplants. Transplants do not necessarily have to take place in the same place as the location of the organ harvesting. The two locations are often different; organs harvested in one place are shipped to another place for transplanting.

The allegation is further that the organs are harvested from the practitioners while they are still alive. The practitioners are killed in the course of the organ harvesting operations or immediately thereafter. These operations are a form of murder. The people killed in this way are then cremated. There is no corpse left to examine to identify as the source of an organ transplant.[20]

Witnessing and the Mark of the Beast

In the midst of this persecution, the alternatives will begin to emerge to either accept the mark of the beast (Revelation 13:10), or give a testimony as a witness for Christ.

> And it shall turn to you for a testimony.

> Settle it therefore in your hearts, not to meditate before what ye shall answer: For I will give you a mouth and wisdom, which all your adversaries shall not be able to gainsay nor resist. Luke 21:13-16.

---

[20] BLOODY HARVEST: Revised Report into Allegations of Organ Harvesting of in China, by David Matas, Esq. and Hon. David Kilgour, Esq., 31 January 2007. http://organharvestinvestigation.net/report0701/rep ort20070131.htm#_Toc160145105

Betrayal

As the man of perdition ascends in the global system, he will cause everyone to worship the beast or the image of the beast and to accept his mark (Revelation 13:10-12). As this pressure rises among the populations of the earth, those still holding to faith in Christ will be betrayed to the forces of the beast by those closest to them:

> And ye shall be betrayed both by parents, and brethren, and kinsfolks, and friends; and some of you shall they cause to be put to death.
> And ye shall be hated of all men for my name's sake. Luke 21:16-17.

Let us make no mistake about it: Many of you are currently attending churches where the congregation claims to be "Christian," yet the church has discipled no one. Many churches preach false gospels,

including gospels of prosperity, salvation by
works, salvation by the intercession of the
saints, and salvation through the practice of
rituals and traditions; the church does not
engage in the holy feasts but instead
practices pagan celebrations including the
worship of Asherah; the church makes no
provision to clothe the naked, feed the
hungry, or to minister to orphans, widows,
and those in prison, but instead, spends every
dollar on church salaries and building
campaigns. The church leadership will not
speak out on issues of the day; instead, the
pastors mealy-mouth sermons designed
expressly to be "seeker friendly" and to fall
squarely within the safe-harbors of their
501(c)(3) tax exemption.

Do not be surprised when the
leadership at your church sells your name to

a government tribunal in a "round up" of Christians.

Blessings

But there shall not an hair of your head perish.

In your patience possess ye your souls. Luke 21:18-19.

Prophecy Concerning the Destruction of Jerusalem

And when ye shall see Jerusalem compassed with armies, then know that the desolation thereof is nigh. Then let them which are in Judaea flee to the mountains; and let them which are in the midst of it depart out; and let not them that are in the countries enter thereinto.

For these be the days of vengeance, that all things which are written may be fulfilled. But woe unto them that are with child, and to them that give suck, in those days! for there

shall be great distress in the land, and
wrath upon this people.

And they shall fall by the edge
of the sword, and shall be led away
captive into all nations: and Jerusalem
shall be trodden down of the Gentiles,
until the times of the Gentiles be
fulfilled.

And there shall be signs in the
sun, and in the moon, and in the stars;
and upon the earth distress of nations,
with perplexity; the sea and the waves
roaring; Men's hearts failing them for
fear, and for looking after those things
which are coming on the earth: for the
powers of heaven shall be shaken.

And then shall they see the Son
of man coming in a cloud with power
and great glory. And when these
things begin to come to pass, then look
up, and lift up your heads; for your
redemption draweth nigh.
-    Luke 21:8-28

PART TWO:

THE IDENTITY OF THE MAN OF LAWLESSNESS

CHAPTER TEN

The man of sin and the son of perdition

2 Thessalonians 2

Now we beseech you, brethren, by the coming of our Lord Jesus Christ, and by our gathering together unto him, 2 Thess. 2:1

This passage opens with a plea to credibility – that is, by the testimony of two witnesses, Paul and his companions known to the Thessalonian church, beseech the congregation to understand what is about to be said.

The two witnesses identified are interesting, because they illustrate the duality of all prophecy, and because this duality is present, the passage is therefore prophetic. Testifying to the truth of this passage is "the coming of our Lord Jesus Christ" and "our gathering together unto him."

The "coming of our Lord Jesus Christ" is of course dual. First, at the time of this prophecy, the coming of the Christ had already occurred, but by the words of Christ, the believers knew that a return was certain.

> And there shall be signs in the sun, and in the moon, and in the stars; and upon the earth distress of nations, with perplexity; the sea and the waves roaring;
> Men's hearts failing them for fear, and for looking after those things which are coming on the earth: for the powers of heaven shall be shaken.
> And then shall they see the Son of man coming in a cloud with power and great glory. Luke 21:25-27.
> And when these things begin to come to pass, then look up, and lift up your heads; for your redemption draweth nigh.

The second witness is the passage our "gathering together unto him." This passage refers first to the fellowship of the believers in the congregation at Thessalonica and other cities, but its duality is found in the gathering of the saints foretold in Revelation.

> After this I beheld, and, lo, a great multitude, which no man could number, of all nations, and kindreds, and people, and tongues, stood before the throne, and before the Lamb, clothed with white robes, and palms in their hands;
> And cried with a loud voice, saying, Salvation to our God which sitteth upon the throne, and unto the Lamb.
> And all the angels stood round about the throne, and about the elders and the four beasts, and fell before the throne on their faces, and worshipped God,
> Saying, Amen: Blessing, and glory, and wisdom, and thanksgiving,

and honour, and power, and might, be unto our God forever and ever. Amen.

And one of the elders answered, saying unto me, What are these which are arrayed in white robes? and whence came they?

And I said unto him, Sir, thou knowest. And he said to me, These are they which came out of great tribulation, and have washed their robes, and made them white in the blood of the Lamb.

Therefore are they before the throne of God, and serve him day and night in his temple: and he that sitteth on the throne shall dwell among them.

They shall hunger no more, neither thirst anymore; neither shall the sun light on them, nor any heat.

For the Lamb which is in the midst of the throne shall feed them, and shall lead them unto living fountains of waters: and God shall wipe away all tears from their eyes. Revelation 7:9-17.

Paul therefore makes a call to credibility based upon two witnesses, both of which have a dual nature. These two witnesses testify as to those things that had already happened, and those things that are to come.

That ye be not soon shaken in mind, or be troubled, neither by spirit, nor by word, nor by letter as from us, as that the day of Christ is at hand. 2 Thess. 2:2

This passage is very straightforward. Paul is telling the church in Thessalonica that the day of Christ is not coming soon. That is the plain meaning of the passage. This passage is a prelude of what is about to be said, establishing the criteria by which they might know when the day of Christ would arrive.

Once again, the dualism of the passage is seen. The readers are directed to not be soon shaken in mind or to be troubled by three things: by spirit, by word or by "letter as from us." The prophecy soon to be set out as to the coming of the day of Christ will then be established by spirit, by word, or by "letter as from us." This time, the number of witnesses is three, not two.

Let no man deceive you by any means: for that day shall not come, except there come a falling away first,

> (But before all these, they shall lay their hands on you, and persecute you, delivering you up to the synagogues, and into prisons, being brought before kings and rulers for my name's sake. Luke 21:12.)

and that man of sin be revealed, the son of perdition; 2 Thess. 2:3

This passage, when joined with the preceding passage, speaks to let no man deceive you (by spirit, word, or letter) by any means. Here is the first prophecy of this section. The deception that will be later described in this passage is a deception that will be in spirit, in word, and in letter.

From here, the prophecy concerning the date of the coming of the day of Christ begins: "for that day shall not come, except there come a falling away first." The inverse of the negative spells out that the day *shall* come but a falling away shall occur first. This is the first time stamp in this prophecy. It has meaning only when construed within all of the other elements of this passage.

The second marker is found in the other half of verse 3: "and that man of sin be revealed, the son of perdition."

Before the day of Christ, the man of sin will "be revealed" and the "son of perdition" will be revealed in the same person.

To best understand this passage, we first need to know a little more about this day of Christ:

> Then if any man shall say unto you, Lo, here is Christ, or there; believe it not.
> For there shall arise false Christs, and false prophets, and shall shew great signs and wonders; insomuch that, if it were possible, they shall deceive the very elect.
> Behold, I have told you before.
> Wherefore if they shall say unto you, Behold, he is in the desert; go not forth: behold, he is in the secret chambers; believe it not.
> For as the lightning cometh out of the east, and shineth even unto the west; so shall also the coming of the Son of man be. Matthew 24:23-27.

The coming of Christ will therefore be a worldwide event. The markers will then also be worldwide. The "falling away" can then be understood as a worldwide falling away. The "man of sin" and the "son of perdition" will be recognized worldwide.

We cannot leave this passage without discussing what is meant by the "man of sin" and what is meant by the "son of perdition."

The Man of Sin

Because "all have sinned and fall short of the glory of God" (Romans 3:23), the man of sin is something more than a man with sin, but a man of sin. Commentators in the past have pointed to Antiochus IV Epiphenes, that man who satisfied all of the prophecy found in Daniel 8:

> And in the latter time of their kingdom [the four kingdoms that

followed Alexander's kingdom], when the transgressors are come to the full, a king of fierce countenance, and understanding dark sentences, shall stand up [Antiochus IV Epiphenes].

And his power shall be mighty [the Seleucid Kingdom was the most powerful of the four kingdoms], but not by his own power [as the son of King Antiochus III the Great, he inherited the kingdom]: and he shall destroy wonderfully, and shall prosper, and practice [in 170 BC, Antiochus launched a preemptive strike against Egypt, conquering all but Alexandria and capturing King Ptolemy], and shall destroy the mighty and the holy people.
- Daniel 8:23-24

When these happenings were reported to the king [A-iv-E], he thought that Judea was in revolt. Raging like a wild animal, he set out from Egypt and took Jerusalem by storm. He ordered his soldiers to cut down without mercy those whom they met and to slay those who took refuge in their houses. There was a massacre of young and old, a killing of women and children, a slaughter of virgins and infants. In the space of three days, eighty thousand were lost, forty thousand meeting a violent death, and the same number being sold into slavery.

- 2 Maccabees 5:11-14.

And through his policy also he shall cause craft to prosper in his hand; and *he shall magnify himself in his heart*, and by peace shall destroy many: he shall also stand up against the prince of princes;

In 168 BC Antiochus led a second attack on Egypt and also sent a fleet to capture Cyprus. Before reaching Alexandria, his path was blocked by a single, old Roman ambassador named Gaius Popillius Laenas, who delivered a message from the Roman Senate directing Antiochus to withdraw his armies from Egypt and Cyprus, or consider themselves in a state of war with the Roman Republic. Antiochus said he would discuss it with his council, whereupon the Roman envoy drew a line in the sand around him and said, "Before you cross this circle I want you to give me a reply for the Roman Senate" - implying that Rome would declare war if the King stepped out of the circle without committing to leave Egypt immediately. Weighing his options, Antiochus wisely decided to withdraw. Only then did Popillius agree to shake hands with him.

but he shall be broken without hand
[Antiochus died suddenly of disease in
164 BC].

- Daniel 8:25

Son of Perdition

The second trait of he who is to be
revealed is that he is a son of perdition. The
phrase "son of perdition" appears in John 17.

> While I was with them in the world, I
> kept them in thy name: those that
> thou gavest me I have kept, and none
> of them is lost, but the son of
> perdition; that the scripture might be
> fulfilled. John 17:12.

Here, the passage is a referral to Judas
Iscariot. The son of perdition is in the literal
sense, Judas Iscariot; however, the one to be
revealed is in the spirit of both Antiochus IV
Epiphenes and Judas Iscariot – two traits, two
witnesses, that will testify to who he is
prophetically.

Judas is discussed throughout the book of John, giving us an idea of the traits that make up a "son of perdition." Judas is several things: he is a betrayer; he is destined for ultimate and eternal destruction; although many may believe that he is a true disciple, the son of perdition is never truly saved; he is never truly a believer; finally, he is considered unclean.

Never truly saved

When Jesus had spoken these words, he went forth with his disciples over the brook Cedron, where was a garden, into which he entered, and his disciples.

And Judas also, which betrayed him, knew the place: for Jesus ofttimes resorted thither with his disciples.

Judas then, having received a band of men and officers from the chief priests and Pharisees, cometh thither with lanterns and torches and weapons.

Jesus therefore, knowing all things that should come upon him, went forth, and said unto them, Whom seek ye?

They answered him, Jesus of Nazareth. Jesus saith unto them, I am he. And Judas also, which betrayed him, stood with them.

As soon then as he had said unto them, I am he, they went backward, and fell to the ground.

Then asked he them again, Whom seek ye? And they said, Jesus of Nazareth.

Jesus answered, I have told you that I am he: if therefore ye seek me, let these go their way:

That the saying might be fulfilled, which he spake, Of them which thou gavest me have I lost none. John 18:1-9.

Never a believer

But there are some of you that believe not. For Jesus knew from the beginning who they were that *believed not,* and who should *betray* him.

And he said, Therefore said I unto you, that no man can come unto me, except it were given unto him of my Father.

From that time many of his disciples went back, and walked no more with him.

Then said Jesus unto the twelve, Will ye also go away?

Then Simon Peter answered him, Lord, to whom shall we go? thou hast the words of eternal life.

And we believe and are sure that thou art that Christ, the Son of the living God.

Jesus answered them, Have not I chosen you twelve, and one of you is a devil?

He spake of Judas Iscariot the son of Simon: for he it was that should betray him, being one of the twelve. John 6:64-71.

Unclean

> Jesus saith to him, He that is
> washed needeth not save to wash his
> feet, but is clean every whit: and ye
> are clean, but not all.
> For he knew who should betray
> him; therefore said he, Ye are not all
> clean. John 13:10-11.

The coming revealed one will also be a
betrayer and one who is destined for ultimate
and eternal destruction. Although many may
believe that he is a true disciple, the son of
perdition is never truly saved, he is never
truly a believer, and he is considered unclean.

Consider a later prophecy:

> And I beheld another beast
> coming up out of the earth; and he had
> two horns like a lamb, and he spake as
> a dragon. Revelation 13:11.

The son of perdition and the beast
that comes up out of the earth have

something in common – people believe they are "like a lamb," but they are not. The lamb is a symbol of Christ, the Lamb of God. The dragon is a symbol of Satan. The beast that comes up out of the earth, then, has the look of Christ, but speaks like Satan. It is noteworthy that the lamb has two horns, when horns don't appear on lambs. Daniel tells us that "horns" means "kings." The two horns therefore indicate two kings. The beast holds two kingship positions that appear Christian – or two Christian kingships, yet speaks with the voice of Satan. He is not a disciple, not truly saved, not a believer, and not clean in the spiritual sense.

To be clean has a particular meaning in the covenant of the blood of Christ:

> Jesus answered and said unto him, If a man love me, he will keep my

words: and my Father will love him, and we will come unto him, and make our abode with him.

He that loveth me not keepeth not my sayings: and the word which ye hear is not mine, but the Father's which sent me.

These things have I spoken unto you, being yet present with you.

But the Comforter, which is the Holy Ghost, whom the Father will send in my name, he shall teach you all things, and bring all things to your remembrance, whatsoever I have said unto you.

Peace I leave with you, my peace I give unto you: not as the world giveth, give I unto you. Let not your heart be troubled, neither let it be afraid. John 14: 23-27.

Now *ye are clean through the word which I have spoken unto you.* John 15:3.

Our man of lawlessness is spiritually a man of sin and a son of perdition:

Man of sin:

- His power shall be mighty, but not by his own power
- He shall destroy wonderfully, and shall prosper, and practice
- He shall destroy the mighty and the holy people (two kingdoms)
- He shall cause craft to prosper in his hand (sorcery)
- He shall magnify himself in his heart
- By peace he shall destroy many
- He shall also stand up against the prince of princes
- He shall be broken without

hand

Son of perdition:

- He does not love Christ
- He does not keep his sayings
- He is not receptive to the Holy Spirit
- He is not at peace
- He is troubled and afraid.

CHAPTER ELEVEN

The criteria of the Man of Lawlessness

Who opposeth and exalteth himself above all that is called God, or that is worshipped; so that he as God sitteth in the temple of God, shewing himself that he is God. 2 Thess. 2:4

Let us begin with how a person might oppose and exalt himself above all that is called God, or that is worshipped. Simply put, it is he who would suppose to judge God. Consider the following statement:

> "Which passage of scripture should guide our public policy? Should we go with Leviticus which suggests slavery is okay? Or we could go with Deuteronomy which suggests stoning your child, or should we just stick to the Sermon on the Mount? a passage that is so radical, that it's doubtful that our own defense

department would survive its application."[21]

The passage from 1 Thessalonians saying that "he shall sit in the temple of God, showing himself that his is God", is another two-fold, or *bifidic* prophecy. One prophecy is a prophecy directed to the *root*, and one directed to the *branch*. To the root, the temple means the so-called third temple, the physical temple that is expected in the end of days. For purposes of clarity: the temple of Solomon was the first and only temple of a united Israel. The second temple was a Judean temple only, built in the province of Judea after the dispersal of the other ten tribes.

---

[21] Barack Hussein Obama

Those of the root still look to the building of a third temple on the temple mount, over the site of the holiest of holies. Those of the branch, have a different understanding:

> What? Know ye not that your body is the temple of the Holy Ghost which is in you, which ye have of God, and ye are not your own?
> For ye are bought with a price: therefore glorify God in your body, and in your spirit, which are God's. 1 Corinthians 6: 19-20.

With the death of Christ on the cross and His subsequent resurrection, the temple is no longer a physical place, but a spiritual place. The passage "he shall sit in the temple of God, showing himself that his is God," is then understood as he who would exalt himself above God in his heart [body] and he who would declare himself the judge over things rightly left to God. Now consider the following example:

"[I define sin as] being out of alignment with my values."[22]

In Christianity, this is the quintessential overthrow of the Holy Spirit in the temple of God, yet such an attitude is now common among the members of modern western civilization.

Sin is defined differently in scripture: "Whosoever commits sin transgresses also the law; for sin is the transgression of the law." 1 John 3:4. *Sin is lawlessness.* "For where there is no law, there is no transgression." Romans 4:15. "Whatever is not from faith is sin." Romans 4:23.

---

[22] Barack Hussein Obama

This self-exaltation is consistent with the prophetic vision found in Daniel 11:

> And the king shall do according to his will; and he shall exalt himself, and magnify himself above every god, and shall speak marvellous things against the God of gods, and shall prosper till the indignation be accomplished: for that that is determined shall be done.
>
> Neither shall he regard the God of his fathers, nor the desire of women, nor regard any god: for he shall magnify himself above all. Daniel 11:36-37.

When the prophecies are merged, we can see a pattern:

- he shall sit in the temple of God
- showing himself that he is God
- he shall do according to his will
- he shall exalt himself

- he shall magnify himself above every god
- he shall speak marvellous things against the God of gods
- he shall prosper till the indignation be accomplished
- he shall not regard the God of his fathers
- he shall not regard the desire of women
- he shall not regard any god
- he shall magnify himself above all

If you join all of these criteria into a simple bundle as above, you can pretty well get the idea about the self-aggrandizing approach of the revealed one.

Consider also that a physical temple will also be built:

How art thou fallen from
heaven, O Lucifer, son of the morning!
how art thou cut down to the ground,
which didst weaken the nations!

For thou hast said in thine
heart, I will ascend into heaven, I will
exalt my throne above the stars of
God: I will sit also upon the mount of
the congregation, in the sides of the
north:

- Isaiah 14:12-13

This appears to be a pretty clear statement that the *Antichrist* of the book of Daniel is the spirit of Lucifer, exalting his throne above the stars of God, and sitting "upon the mount of the congregation, in the sides of the north."

We will discuss this throne of Satan in more detail in the next chapter, however, this passage indicates that the throne of Satan is likely to be placed "upon the mount of the congregation," just before Satan is cast down:

> Yet thou shalt be brought down to hell, to the sides of the pit.
>
> They that see thee shall narrowly look upon thee, and consider thee, saying, Is this the man that made the earth to tremble, that did shake kingdoms;
>
> That made the world as a wilderness, and destroyed the cities thereof; that opened not the house of his prisoners?
>
> All the kings of the nations, even all of them, lie in glory, everyone in his own house.
>
> But thou art cast out of thy grave like an abominable branch, and as the raiment of those that are slain, thrust through with a sword, that go down to the stones of the pit; as a carcase trodden under feet.
>
> - Isaiah 14:15-19

Now, consider more of the prophecy in Daniel 11:

> But in his estate shall he honour the God of forces: and a god whom his fathers knew not shall he honour with gold, and silver, and with precious stones, and pleasant things. Thus shall he do in the most strong holds with a strange god, whom he shall acknowledge and increase with glory: and he shall cause them to rule over many, and shall divide the land for gain. Daniel 11:38-39.

Here, the vision is that this king shall honor the God of forces (fortresses in the NKJV, NAS, NIV, ESV). He honors a god of war. Now consider another example on the application of scripture in the making of public policy, and notice the exaltation of the defense department above the teachings of the Sermon on the Mount.

> "Which passage of scripture should guide our public policy? Should we go with Leviticus which suggests slavery is okay? Or we could go with Deuteronomy which suggests stoning your child, or should we just stick to the Sermon on the Mount? a passage that is so radical, that it's doubtful that our own defense department would survive its application."

Remember ye not, that, when I was yet with you, I told you these things? 2 Thess. 2:5.

Paul references that prophecy was something he discussed with the church in Thessalonica when he was there. In particular, Paul must have discussed those things related to the revealing of the man of lawlessness. The importance of prophecy is stressed by Paul in other writings as well.

> Pursue love, and desire spiritual *gifts,* but especially that you may prophesy. For he who speaks in a tongue does not speak to men but to God, for no one understands *him;* however, in the spirit he speaks mysteries. But he who prophesies speaks edification and exhortation and comfort to men. He who speaks in a tongue edifies himself, but he who prophesies edifies the church. I wish you all spoke with tongues, but even more that you prophesied; for he who prophesies *is* greater than he who speaks with tongues, unless indeed he interprets, that the church may receive edification. 1 Corinthians 14:1-5.

Additional criteria:

- He shall honor the God of forces/fortresses.
- He shall honor a god whom his fathers knew not with gold, and

silver, and with precious
stones, and pleasant things.
- He shall be in the most strong
holds with a strange god,
whom he shall acknowledge
and increase with glory.
- He shall rule over many,
- He shall divide the land for
gain. Daniel 11:38-39.

This term "fortresses" has additional
meaning, when you consider its application
in the Russian language. One kind of fortress
in Russia, such as the walled fortress
surrounding the buildings of government in
Moscow, is called a *kremlin* (the Moscow
fortress is known as *the* Kremlin). Consider
the prophecy now in replacement: he shall
honor the god of the Kremlin. In front of the
Kremlin is the tomb of Vladimir Lenin – the
god of communism. Our man of lawlessness

honors this god, Vladimir Lenin, and his theology, communism.

In addition, Obama announced to the UN his desire for a "contiguous Palestinian state." He now pushes for the division of Jerusalem – dividing the land for gain.

This summarizes those things found in 2 Thessalonians 2 that we may look to in order that we might establish the day of Christ, and the revealing of the man of lawlessness.

CHAPTER TWELVE

The time of the man of lawlessness

And now ye know what withholdeth that he might be revealed in his time. 2 Thessalonians 2:6

The key to this passage lies in the last of the phrase: "that he might be revealed in his time." To understand this, we must return to the words of Christ in the parable of the fig tree, also found in Luke 21:'

> Then He spoke to them a parable: "Look at the fig tree, and all the trees. When they are already budding, you see and know for yourselves that summer is now near. So you also, when you see these things happening, know that the kingdom of God is near. Assuredly, I say to you, this generation will by no means pass away till all things take place. Heaven and earth will pass away, but My

words will by no means pass away. Luke 21:29-33.

This prophecy speaks of a fig tree. There is much to say about the fig tree in scripture, and it is worthy of a review.

> I looked when He opened the sixth seal, and behold, there was a great earthquake; and the sun became black as sackcloth of hair, and the moon became like blood. And the stars of heaven fell to the earth, as a fig tree drops its late figs when it is shaken by a mighty wind. Then the sky receded as a scroll when it is rolled up, and every mountain and island was moved out of its place. And the kings of the earth, the great men, the rich men, the commanders, the mighty men, every slave and every free man, hid themselves in the caves and in the rocks of the mountains, and said to the mountains and rocks, "Fall on us and hide us from the face of Him who sits on the throne and from the wrath of the Lamb! For the great day

of His wrath has come, and who is able to stand?" Revelation 6:12-17.

Now compare with the statement made in Isaiah.

> All the host of heaven shall be dissolved, And the heavens shall be rolled up like a scroll; All their host shall fall down As the leaf falls from the vine, And as *fruit* falling from a fig tree. Isaiah 34:4.

Consider also the statement made concerning the unified kingdoms under Solomon in 1 Kings.

> For he had dominion over all *the region* on this side of the River from Tiphsah even to Gaza, namely over all the kings on this side of the River; and he had peace on every side all around him. And Judah and Israel dwelt safely, each man under his vine and his fig tree, from Dan as far as

Beersheba, all the days of Solomon. 1
Kings 4:24-25.

The Old Testament discusses the both
the vine and the fig tree, yet when the
testimony of the blood covenant of Christ
begins, the discussion moves only to the fig
tree. The importance of this change has to do
the revealing of the vine.

> "I am the true vine, and My
> Father is the vinedresser. Every
> branch in Me that does not bear fruit
> He takes away; and every *branch* that
> bears fruit He prunes, that it may bear
> more fruit. You are already clean
> because of the word which I have
> spoken to you. Abide in Me, and I in
> you. As the branch cannot bear fruit of
> itself, unless it abides in the vine,
> neither can you, unless you abide in
> Me.
> "I am the vine, you *are* the
> branches. He who abides in Me, and I
> in him, bears much fruit; for without
> Me you can do nothing. If anyone does

not abide in Me, he is cast out as a branch and is withered; and they gather them and throw *them* into the fire, and they are burned. If you abide in Me, and My words abide in you, you will ask what you desire, and it shall be done for you. By this My Father is glorified, that you bear much fruit; so you will be My disciples. John 15:1-8.

The vine – the true vine – is the abidance in Christ. In the traditions before the birth of Christ, faith in the Messiah and the promise of redemption through the sacrifice of Christ on the cross and His subsequent resurrection connected "each man to his vine."

The fig tree is different. Because the fruits from the fig tree are the manifest actions of men, so the fig tree itself is best understood as the mores, customs, practices, and traditions of the given social order. The phrase found in 1 Kings 4 "[a]nd Judah and Israel dwelt safely, each man under his vine and his fig tree, from Dan as far as Beersheba, all the days of Solomon" can then be understood as each of the two kingdoms Judah and Israel (the southern and northern kingdoms respectively) dwelt safely, each man connected to his God, and each man living under the mores, customs, practices and traditions found in his kingdom. This same passage has a prophetic side as well, indicating that with the revealing of the true vine, those who did not abide in Him were left only with mores, customs, practices and traditions.

The passage in Isaiah also reveals prophecy, saying that "All the host of heaven shall be dissolved, And the heavens shall be rolled up like a scroll; All their host shall fall down As the leaf falls from the vine, And as *fruit* falling from a fig tree." Angels shall fall from heaven, as those who were intended to abide in Christ fall away, and as the traditions of men come to fruition as set forth in Luke 21.

Let's review what fruits of mankind's traditions become:

- Nation will rise against nation, and kingdom against kingdom;
- There will be great earthquakes in various places;
- There will be famines and pestilences;
- There will be fearful sights and great signs from heaven;
- They will lay their hands on you and persecute *you;*

- They will deliver *you* up to the synagogues and prisons;
- You will be brought before kings and rulers for My name's sake;
- It will turn out for you as an occasion for testimony;
- You will be betrayed even by parents and brothers, relatives and friends;
- They will put *some* of you to death;
- You will be hated by all for My name's sake;
- Not a hair of your head shall be lost;
- By your patience possess your souls.

When we consider the parable of the fig tree, we begin to see the timing of this.

"Look at the fig tree, and all the trees." We are then told to look at the mores, customs, practices and traditions of men, both in Israel and at all other nations.

"When they are already budding, you see and know for yourselves that summer is now near. So you also, when you see these things happening, know that the kingdom of God is near." When you see nations and kingdoms turn against one another (a destruction of the idea of the family of sovereign nations), when great earthquakes are seen in diverse places (not the usual places and in many places), when famines and plagues rise throughout the nations and kingdoms (flu virus, bubonic plague), when great signs are seen in the heavens, and when

Christian persecution is present in nations and kingdoms, the fruit on the fig tree will be ripe, signaling the time of the day of Christ. This worldwide persecution of Christians is referred to by Paul in his reference to the "falling away" in 2 Thessalonians 2, an understanding he taught while he was there.

How long will this take, from the appearance of the budding on the fig trees until the culmination? "Assuredly, I say to you, this generation will by no means pass away till all things take place. Heaven and earth will pass away, but My words will by no means pass away." Luke 21:32-33.

The mores, customs, practices and traditions of the united kingdom of Solomon must first return for the fig tree analogy to have any meaning. The creation of the Judean Kingdom and the second temple does not qualify, because the rise of the Maccabean kingdom was a kingdom only of the remaining tribes – Judah and Levi, as the other ten tribes had been dispersed following the Assyrian destruction in 609 BC, and the second temple only a temple for the Judean kingdom.

Only the recreation of the nation of Israel by means of the 1947 decree, and the declaration of sovereignty in 1948 can qualify. "The days of our lives *are* seventy years." Psalm 90:10. This prophecy then delivers a specific timing. The budding begins with the establishment of the "fig tree" in 1947, and its fruit will be ripe within seventy years, or by 2017.

Let us consider those fruits:

> "But when you see Jerusalem surrounded by armies, then know that

its desolation is near. Then let those who are in Judea flee to the mountains, let those who are in the midst of her depart, and let not those who are in the country enter her. For these are the days of vengeance, that all things which are written may be fulfilled. But woe to those who are pregnant and to those who are nursing babies in those days! For there will be great distress in the land and wrath upon this people. And they will fall by the edge of the sword, and be led away captive into all nations. And Jerusalem will be trampled by Gentiles until the times of the Gentiles are fulfilled.

"And there will be signs in the sun, in the moon, and in the stars; and on the earth distress of nations, with perplexity, the sea and the waves roaring; men's hearts failing them from fear and the expectation of those things which are coming on the earth, for the powers of the heavens will be shaken. Then they will see the Son of Man coming in a cloud with power and great glory. Now when these things begin to happen, look up and lift up your heads, because your redemption draws near." Luke 21:20-28.

When we consider such time, that the man of lawlessness "might be revealed in his time," consider that "what withholdeth" as described in Daniel 12:

> And he said, "Go *your way,* Daniel, for the words *are* closed up and sealed till the time of the end. Daniel 12:9.

The seal referenced in Daniel 12:9 is that "what withhodeth." The seal is opened, however, when the United Nations adopted Resolution 181 on November 29, 1947 to rebuild Jerusalem.

CHAPTER THIRTEEN

The revealing of the man of lawlessness

For the mystery of iniquity [*lawlessness* ESB, NKJV, NIV, NASB] doth already work: only he who now letteth will let, until he be taken out of the way.
2 Thess. 2:7.

This passage from 2 Thessalonians 2 is also a prophetic dating, but a dating that can only be understood *propter hoc*. The mystery of iniquity begins with the fall of man, the falling away from God when Eve ate from the tree of the knowledge of good and evil, and when Adam approved and followed.

> So when the woman saw that the tree *was* good for food, that it *was* pleasant to the eyes, and a tree desirable to make *one* wise, she took of its fruit and ate. She also gave to her husband with her, and he ate. Then the eyes of both of them were opened,

and they knew that they *were* naked; and they sewed fig leaves together and made themselves coverings. Genesis 3:6-7.

The mystery of iniquity is that mystery that brought death into the world.

Wherefore, as by one man sin entered into the world, and death by sin; and so death passed upon all men, for that all have sinned. Romans 5:12.

John Wesley, in his Sermon 61 (text from the 1872 edition - Thomas Jackson, editor), preached that the mystery of iniquity was "the energy of Satan," and we can see that the mystery of iniquity is the energy of Satan, sin, and the effects of sin – man's separation from God.

As this passage continues we discover the dating aspect of this prophecy, where "only he who now letteth will let, until he be taken out of the way." Satan's working in driving this mystery of iniquity will be "taken out of the way" at the time of the rise of the lawless one.

And then shall that Wicked [*lawless one* ESB, NKJV, NIV, NASB] be revealed, whom the Lord shall consume with the spirit of his mouth, and shall destroy with the brightness of his coming: 2 Thess. 2:8

The center point of this prophecy is found in this passage, because again, we find a truth claim "and then shall that lawless one be revealed," and the testimony of two witnesses to confirm his identity: 1) the Lord shall consume him with the spirit of his mouth; and 2) he shall be destroyed with the brightness of his coming.

Although these are *propter hoc*, or *a posteriori* witnesses, allowing us to determine the identity of the lawless one only after his being consumed and being destroyed, these witnesses are necessary to proclaim both the ultimate victory of Christ and the means by which this lawless one will be destroyed – by the spirit of the mouth of the Lord, and with the brightness of his coming.

Even him, whose coming is after the working of Satan with all power and signs and lying wonders, and with all deceivableness of unrighteousness in them that perish; because they received not the love of the truth, that they might be saved. 2 Thess. 2:9-10.

Here we have specificity that the lawless one is a "him" whose coming is after the working of Satan – meaning that his working is like the working of Satan, and that he will arrive after the working of Satan (Satan's hand in the mystery of iniquity).

This lawless one will come "with all power and signs and lying wonders and with all deceivableness of unrighteousness". This agrees with what is said concerning the beast that rises from the earth in Revelation 13.

> He performs great signs, so that he even makes fire come down from heaven on the earth in the sight of men. And he deceives those who dwell on the earth by those signs which he was granted to do in the sight of the beast, telling those who dwell on the earth to make an image to the beast who was wounded by the sword and lived. Revelation 13:13-14.

"He even makes fire come down from heaven on the earth in the sight of men" is a reference to the great signs of Elijah:

> Then the king sent to him a captain of fifty with his fifty men. So he went up to him; and there he was, sitting on the top of a hill. And he spoke to him: "Man of God, the king

has said, 'Come down!'" So Elijah answered and said to the captain of fifty, "If I *am* a man of God, then let fire come down from heaven and consume you and your fifty men." And fire came down from heaven and consumed him and his fifty. Then he sent to him another captain of fifty with his fifty men. And he answered and said to him: "Man of God, thus has the king said, 'Come down quickly!'" So Elijah answered and said to them, "If I *am* a man of God, let fire come down from heaven and consume you and your fifty men." And the fire of God came down from heaven and consumed him and his fifty. 2 Kings 1:9-12.

However, 2 Thessalonians 2 tells us that such performances are "signs and lying wonders" performed with all deceivableness of unrighteousness." Unlike Elijah, these signs performed by the man of lawlessness will be false. This is affirmed in the prophecy of Revelation 13, when it speaks that "he deceives those who dwell on the earth by those signs which he was granted to do in the sight of the beast."

Because he has deceived those who dwell on the earth, and because they have believed his lies, he then tells those who dwell on the earth to make an image to the beast who was wounded by the sword and lived.   This too is a lying wonder and a great sign.

And for this cause God shall send them strong delusion, that they should believe a lie:
That they all might be damned who believed not the truth, but had pleasure in unrighteousness. 2 Thessalonians 2:11.

Certainly this is one of the most profound prophecies in all of scripture. The reason God sends them a strong delusion is because they did not believe the truth and had pleasure in unrighteousness. This pleasure in unrighteousness is set forth in greater detail in Paul's letters to the Romans:

> For the wrath of God is revealed from heaven against all ungodliness and unrighteousness of men, who suppress the truth in unrighteousness, because what may be known of God is manifest in them, for God has shown *it* to them. For since the creation of the world His invisible *attributes* are clearly seen, being understood by the things that are made, *even* His eternal power and Godhead, so that they are without excuse, because, although they knew God, they did not glorify *Him* as God, nor were thankful, but became futile in their thoughts, and their foolish hearts were darkened. Professing to be wise, they became fools, and changed the glory of the incorruptible God into an image made like corruptible man—and birds and four-footed animals and creeping things. Therefore God also gave them

up to uncleanness, in the lusts of their hearts, to dishonor their bodies among themselves, who exchanged the truth of God for the lie, and worshiped and served the creature rather than the Creator, who is blessed forever. Amen.

For this reason God gave them up to vile passions. For even their women exchanged the natural use for what is against nature. Likewise also the men, leaving the natural use of the woman, burned in their lust for one another, men with men committing what is shameful, and receiving in themselves the penalty of their error which was due.

And even as they did not like to retain God in *their* knowledge, God gave them over to a debased mind, to do those things which are not fitting; being filled with all unrighteousness, sexual immorality, wickedness, covetousness, maliciousness; full of envy, murder, strife, deceit, evil-mindedness; *they are* whisperers, backbiters, haters of God, violent, proud, boasters, inventors of evil things, disobedient to parents, undiscerning, untrustworthy, unloving, unforgiving, unmerciful; who, knowing the righteous judgment of God, that those who practice such things are deserving of death, not only do the same but also approve of those who practice them. Romans 1:18-32.

Paul gives us another list of unrighteousness as well in his first letter to the Corinthians:

Do you not know that the unrighteous will not inherit the kingdom of God? Do not be deceived. Neither fornicators, nor idolaters, nor adulterers, nor homosexuals, nor sodomites, nor thieves, nor covetous, nor drunkards, nor revilers, nor extortioners will inherit the kingdom of God. 1 Corinthians 6:9-10.

These lists are not set forth here in order to garner the ire of the Canadian Human Rights Commission (who believes that the bible is *per se* sexual discrimination), but to identify those who will be damned to believe the lies of the lawless one, to believe the delusion that God is sending.

First on the list are "those who refused to believe the truth." Although I could write an additional book on this issue of truth, I will summarize this issue as follows:

> Pilate therefore said to Him, "Are You a king then?"
> Jesus answered, "You say *rightly* that I am a king. For this cause I was born, and for this cause I have come into the world, that I should bear witness to the truth. Everyone who is of the truth hears My voice."
> Pilate said to Him, "What is truth?" And when he had said this, he went out again to the Jews, and said to them, "I find no fault in Him at all. John 18:37-38.

The question "what is truth?" is that question that when answered determines the course of human history in any given civil society. This is the very center of righteousness (correctness) – the proper identification of that which is (the truth). We are able to establish the truth of a matter by the testimony of two or more witnesses.

> "*By the mouth of two or three witnesses every word may be established.*' Matthew 18:16, Deuteronomy 19:15.

The truth claims set forth in the bible are fundamentally the testimony of two witnesses: the old witness (the Old Testament) and the new witness (the New Testament). As it has been said, the Old Testament is the New Testament concealed, and the New Testament is the Old Testament revealed. This relationship is referenced in Jeremiah 11, Romans 11 and Revelation 11, telling us of the Olive tree, the root and the branch.

Let us now consider the truth claim which has given division on earth (Luke 12:51).

> Jesus said to him, "I am the way, the truth, and the life. No one comes to the Father except through Me." John 14:6.

Ultimately, those who reject this truth claim – that Jesus is the way, the truth, and the life – are those who will be given over to great delusion, to believe a lie that they might perish.

> And Jesus answered and said unto them, Take heed that no man deceive you. For many shall come in my name, saying, I am Christ; and shall deceive many. Luke 21:4-5.

The lawless will do great signs, with all power and signs and lying wonders and with all deceivableness of unrighteousness, that will be believed by those given over to delusion, to believe these lies that they might perish. Here are some examples:

referring to Obama

" ... a light will shine through that window, a beam of light will come down upon you, you will experience an epiphany ..." January 7, 2008.

"No one saw him coming, and Christians believe God comes at us from strange angles and places we don't expect, like Jesus being born in a manger." Lawrence Carter, 2008.

"Many even see in him a messiah-like figure, a great soul, and some affectionately call him Mahatma." Dinesh Sharma, 2008.

"We just like to say his name. We are considering taking it as a mantra." Chicago Sun-Times, 2008.

"A Lightworker – An Attuned Being with Powerful Luminoisty and High-Vibration Integrity who will actually help usher in a New Way of Being." Mark Morford, 2008.

"He communicates God-like energy . . ." Steve Davis, 2008.

"Not just an ordinary human being but indeed an Advanced Soul." Commentator@Chicago Sun-Times, 2008.

"He is the agent of transformation in an age of revolution, as a figure uniquely qualified to open the door to the 21st century." Gary —Hart, 2008.

"He is our collective representation of our purest hopes, our highest visions and our deepest knowings . . .he's our product out of the all-knowing quantum field of intelligence." Eve Konstantine, 2008.

"This is the New Testament." *lost* → Chris Matthews, 2008.

"His finest speeches do not excite. They do not inform. They don't even really inspire. They elevate . . . he is not the Word made flesh, *but the triumph of word over flesh*." Ezra Klein, 2008.

"He has the capacity to summon heroic forces from the spiritual depths of ordinary citizens and to unleash therefrom a symphonic chorus of unique creative acts whose common purpose is to tame the soul and alleviate the great challenges." Gerald Campbell, 2008.

"I would characterize [his rise as] blessed and highly favored. That's not routine. There's something else going on. I think [it] was divinely ordered . . . I know that that was God's plan." Bill Rush, 2008.

"I have thrown myself into a new world – one in which fluffy chatter and frivolous praise are replaced by disciple-like devotion . . ." Samantha Fennell, 2008.

"Everything's going to be affected by this seismic change in the universe." Spike Lee, 2008.

"He won't just heal our city-states and souls. He won't just bring the Heavenly Kingdom – dreamt of in both Platonism and Christianity – to earth. He will heal the earth itself." Micah Tillman, 2008.[23]

Now consider that which will follow the lying signs and wonders, the deception and the delusion:

He was granted *power* to give breath to the image of the beast, that

---

[23] http://obamamessiah.blogspot.com/

the image of the beast should both speak and cause as many as would not worship the image of the beast to be killed. He causes all, both small and great, rich and poor, free and slave, to receive a mark on their right hand or on their foreheads, and that no one may buy or sell except one who has the mark or the name of the beast, or the number of his name. Revelation 13:15-17.

It might be worth your time to know what is the mark or the name of the beast.

CHAPTER FOURTEEN

The beast coming up out of the earth

Let us now discover if this man of lawlessness is also the "beast coming up out of the earth" as described in Revelation 13.

> And I beheld another beast coming up out of the earth; and he had two horns like a lamb, and he spake as a dragon. Revelation 13:11.

Assyrian Pagan God holding a lamb with horns.

First, this "coming up out of the earth"
is an indication that this beast is a man:

> In the sweat of thy face shalt
> thou eat bread, till thou return unto
> **the ground; for out of it wast thou
> taken**: for dust thou art, and unto dust
> shalt thou return. Genesis 3:19.

This man will then be understood by
additional criteria: He will have two horns,
which is to say, he will hold two *kingships*,
both of which shall appear as the lamb – as
sacrificial or servant positions ("like a lamb"),
but he will speak "like a dragon," which is to
say he will deceive with his words. ("And the
great dragon was cast out, that old serpent,
called the Devil, and Satan, which deceiveth
the whole world: he was cast out into the
earth, and his angels were cast out with him."
Revelation 12:9).

This man will exercise the power of the "first beast."

> And I stood upon the sand of the sea, and saw a beast rise up out of the sea, having seven heads and ten horns, and upon his horns ten crowns, and upon his heads the name of blasphemy. Revelation 13:1.

He will then cause those who dwell on the earth to worship this first beast. Revelation 13:12. To make a determination as to whom this might be, we need to first determine the identity of this first beast.

> Then another sign appeared in heaven: an enormous red dragon with seven heads and ten horns and seven crowns on his heads. Revelation 12:3.

> Then the angel carried me away in the Spirit into a desert. There I saw a woman sitting on a scarlet beast that was covered with

blasphemous names and had seven heads and ten horns. Revelation 17:3.

Then I wanted to know the true meaning of the fourth beast, which was different from all the others and most terrifying, with its iron teeth and bronze claws--the beast that crushed and devoured its victims and trampled underfoot whatever was left. I also wanted to know about the ten horns on its head and about the other horn that came up, before which three of them fell--the horn that looked more imposing than the others and that had eyes and a mouth that spoke boastfully. As I watched, this horn was waging war against the saints and defeating them, until the Ancient of Days came and pronounced judgment in favor of the saints of the Most High, and the time came when they possessed the kingdom. Daniel 7:19-22.

We are given the definition within the Word of God of "horns" and "heads:"

The ten horns are ten kings who will come from this kingdom. After them another king will arise, different from the earlier ones; he will subdue three kings. Daniel 7:24.

And here is the mind which hath wisdom. The seven heads are seven *mountains*, on which the woman sitteth. And there are seven kings: five are fallen, and one is, and the other is not yet come; and when he cometh, he must continue a short space. And the beast that was, and is not, even he is the eighth, and is of the seven, and goeth into perdition. And the ten horns which thou sawest are ten kings, which have received no kingdom as yet; but receive power as kings one hour with the beast. These have one mind, and shall give their power and strength unto the beast. Revelation 17:9-13.

The seven heads and ten horns are referred to as two separate parts of the whole. The reason that these are always referenced in this manner is that they will never fully blend into a single unit. Let us consider who they might be. Consider that, in Islamic eschatology, there is an expectation that the Mahdi will come to power immediately following a peace treaty brokered by a Jew from the priesthood of Aaron between the Arabs and the "Romans," (now, the modern EU, or the West) and will be upheld for seven years.

Let us then assume that one side of this beast is of the Arab world, and one side is of the Roman world. Consider also that the beast coming up out of the earth holds two kingships – that the authority he holds is authority from both the Arab world and the Roman world.

This prophecy about "the beast that rises out of the sea" is also consistent with

Islamic prophecy, claiming that the Mahdi – the Muslim Twelfth Imam - will also come to rule the Muslim and non-Muslim world together. He is expected to fight against the forces of evil, lead a world revolution and set up *a new world order* based on justice, righteousness and virtue . . . ultimately taking the world administration in his hands and making Islam victorious over all the religions.

We are told that this beast which rises out of the earth "causeth all, both small and great, rich and poor, free and bond, to receive a mark in their right hand, or in their foreheads: And that no man might buy or sell, save he that had the mark, or the name of the beast, or the number of his name." Revelation 13:16-17. The ability to function in commerce will then depend on whether the mark of the beast has been received.

The beast out of the sea could therefore be a *banking* or *financial* coalition of the G7/8 and OAPEC, replete with an international agreed currency and an international central bank. For this bank to be Islamic in nature, it must be based on Sharia financing principles, not the banking principles of infidels. All those who dwell on the earth will be forced to accept Sharia if they expect to buy or sell. For those of you who have believed that such a mark will be a bar code, or a subcutaneous microchip using bar code identifiers may not be far from the mark, although the receiving of the mark "in their right hand," means *acting on* the belief, and receiving the mark "in their foreheads" means *believing* that it is true, and believing in the beast.

If Sharia is the mark of the beast, then the beast must be an Islamic coalition. There are many reasons to believe this, which will be discussed in the next chapter. What is important to understand here is that "the beast which rises out of the earth" will in turn cause "all, both small and great, rich and poor, free and bond," to worship the first beast and to receive the mark of the beast.

For those who think this is far-fetched, consider the following roster of Sharia Compliant Banks: Alpha Natural Resources; Asset Acceptance Capital Corporation; Aviva Plc; AXA; Barclays PLC; BNP Paribas Group; Citibank, N.A.; Credit Agricole, S.A.; Deutsche Bank AG; Dow Jones & Company Inc.; Equity Insurance Group Limited; Goldman Sachs Group; HBOS plc; HSBC Holdings plc; INVESCO Perpetual; Julius Baer Group;

Maersk Logistics; Merrill Lynch & Co., Inc.;
Morgan Stanley; NYSE Euronext ; Silicon
Graphics, Inc.; Singapore Power; and Bank
Negara Malaysia (The central bank of
Malaysia).

> And he doeth great wonders, so
> that he maketh fire come down from
> heaven on the earth in the sight of
> men, And deceiveth them that dwell
> on the earth by the means of those
> miracles which he had power to do in
> the sight of the beast; saying to them
> that dwell on the earth, that they
> should make an image to the beast,
> which had the wound by a sword, and
> did live. Revelation 13:13-14.

The beast that rises out of the earth
shall then say "to them that dwell on the
earth, that they should make an image to the
beast, which had the wound by a sword, and
did live." It will be this man of lawlessness,
this beast that rises out of the sea, this Mahdi

that will tell those who dwell on the earth to create this "image" to the beast. It will be his recommendation.

Consider this symbol:

On July 10, 2009, Russian President Dmitri Medvedev unveiled this sample coin of the proposed World Currency at the G-7/8 summit in L'Aquila, Italy, calling it "a good sign."

http://www.suijurisclub.net/end-america/5180-medvedev-shows-off-sample-coin-new-world-currency-g-8-a.html.

Now consider the recommendation to institute a new, international currency which would stop the collapse of currencies worldwide by means of fixing the exchange rate by the edict of a new, international authority created by the coalition of OAPEC and the G7/8, including an international central bank, and an international executive branch to compliment the international criminal court at the Hague, the International Court of Human Rights in Strasburg, France, the International Civil Court in Brussels, Belgium, and the International Parliament we currently call the United Nations in New York. The coin you see above is the new proposed currency for international finance, which will exist primarily in the digital/virtual world, and which will be regulated pursuant to Islamic or Sharia financing principles.

> And he had power to give life unto the image of the beast, that the image of the beast should both speak and cause that as many as would not worship the image of the beast should be killed. Revelation 13:15.

Consider that this image of the beast is the concept, the idea, of the beast for world domination. This image of the beast is this joint coalition of western secularism and radical Islam – it is a marriage of the concepts of "sustainable development," "global warming," and Islamic Nazism. In short, it is a beast that intends to destroy most of humanity under its leadership.

The man who is the beast that rises from the earth gives life to this idea, - in fact, it is his idea - and he causes the idea to have a voice in world affairs, most likely by means of propaganda through the electronic media. He also forces people to accept the idea – a Nazi-like idea of Islamism – or suffer the consequences which would be death. In private circles within secular Turkey, the rallying cry of such Islamic national socialism is "önce vattan" – motherland first. Now, travel by GoogleEarth to that place where Satan has his throne and where Satan dwells (Revelation 2:13) and see for yourself.

You may ask yourself if this is at all possible. Consider this most recent news item:

Kissinger: Obama primed to create 'New World Order'

According to Henry Kissinger, the Nobel Peace Prize winner and former secretary of state under President Nixon, conflicts across the globe and an international respect for Barack Obama have created the perfect setting for establishment of "a New World Order."

Kissinger made the remark in an interview with CNBC's "Squawk on the Street" hosts Mark Haines and Erin Burnett at the New York Stock Exchange, after Burnett asked him what international conflict would define the Obama administration's foreign policy.

"There is a need for a new world order," Kissinger told PBS interviewer Charlie Rose last year, "I think that at the end of this administration, with all its turmoil, and at the beginning of the next, we might actually witness the creation of a new order – because people *looking in the abyss*, even in the Islamic world, have to conclude that at some point, *ordered expectations must return under a different system*."

Kissinger was also part of last year's super-secret Bilderberg Group, an organization of powerful international elites, including government, business, academic and journalistic representatives, that has convened annually since 1954.

According to sources that have penetrated the high-security meetings in the past, the Bilderberg meetings emphasize a globalist agenda and promote the idea that the notion of national sovereignty is antiquated and regressive.

CNBC's Haines concluded the Kissinger interview by asking, "Are you confident about the people President-elect Obama has chosen to surround him?"

Kissinger replied, "He has appointed an extraordinarily able group of people in both the *international and financial* fields."[24]

The man who is the beast that rises

from the earth who gives life to the idea of

---

[24] Kissinger: Obama primed to create "New World Order", WorldNetDaily, Drew Zahn, January 6, 2009. http://www.wnd.com/index.php?fa=PAGE.view&page Id=85442

the image of the beast does other things as well:

> And he causeth all, both small and great, rich and poor, free and bond, to receive a mark in their right hand, or in their foreheads: And that no man might buy or sell, save he that had the mark, or the name of the beast, or the number of his name. Revelation 13:16-17.

Some of us may ask the question as to what this mark on the forehead might be. Some people picture a 666 tattooed on the forehead. But consider the following passage from the Quran:

> You may see them kneeling and bowing in reverence, seeking His favor and acceptance. *Their mark is on their foreheads* from the effect of prostrations. Quran, 48:29.

To finish the prophecy, let us finally consider that infamous number that has been assigned to villains and nemeses over the centuries.

> Here is wisdom. Let him that hath understanding count the number of the beast: for it is the number of a man; and his number is Six hundred threescore and six. Revelation 13:18.

Numerology is not my subject, nor should it be. The reader should keep in mind, however, that Arabic people developed the concept of the zero, and numerology is a subject held dear in the Islamic world. The prophecy explains that the number is "the number of a man." Islam is interesting as a religion, because Muhammad never held himself out as God – only as the one true prophet of Allah, the name of the Muslim god. Muhammad is said to be the author of the Quran by word if not by writing. His writing that is the Quran could therefore be the number of the man Muhammad, if it in fact has a number.

The Quran does have a number, and its number is considered to be the mystical number of the Quran. The Quran is divided into a series of books or maybe poems (some are as short as a few lines) called Surahs. The Quran contains 114 Surahs. 114 has a numerological number, which is the sum of all of the numerological extrapolations of the number 114. Let us now consider what they might be: 1-1-4, 4-1-1, and 1-4-1. Simple addition is all that is necessary. 114 + 411 + 141 = 666. You will note that this number is not six, then six, and then six. It is "six hundred threescore and six" – there's a difference.

However, the number six hundred three score and six is based upon the Greek letters Kai, Psi, and Stigma, each letter receiving a number in the original Greek - six hundred, sixty and six respectively. However, in the original text, the letters appear to be Kai, Psi, and Stigma. Walid Shoebat points out that the letters appear to be more Arabic letters rather than Greek letters. If so, the meaning is "in the name of Allah."

> Here is wisdom. Let him that hath understanding count the number of the beast: for it is the number of a man; and his number is Six hundred threescore and six.
> - Revelation 13:8
> -

The Greek word translated here as "number" is arithmos (αριθνος), which actually means the "unknown number". Now consider the passage: "Let him that hath understanding count the unknown number of the beast: for it is the unknown number of a man; and his unknown number is Kai, Psi, and Stigma."

Now consider an application which renders the last three letters as "in the name of Allah" and which construes the "unknown number" as the *multitude*: "Let him that hath understanding count the multitude of the beast; for it is the multitude of a man; and his multitude is "in the name of Allah." Consider that the man referenced is a successor to Muhammad. Once again, the finger points directly at Islam.

Let's review:

- *The beast which rises out of the sea*, is an international coalition between the G7/8 and OAPEC, which creates an international currency, an International Central

Bank, and ultimately, an International Government which joins the banking system with pre-existing international courts and the United Nations, imposing Sharia practices on the worldwide system.

- *The beast which rises out of the earth,* is a man who holds two kingships, lies and deceives, does great but false wonders, deceives everyone on earth, requires worship of the image of the beast from the sea, gives life to its image, and causes those who refuse to so worship to be killed. He also causes everyone who wishes to buy or sell to receive the mark of the beast if they do not carry the name of the beast, the mark of the beast or the number of the beast on their right hand or forehead.

- The image of the beast created by men is a man-made idol which is to be worshipped, such as the dollar.
- The image of the beast created by the man is an idea – a philosophy, a civil morality, a worldwide civil order.

Given these prophecies and given what we are about to learn about the dates in the book of Daniel which have been unsealed, as that which withholdeth has been taken out of the way, we can conclude that:

- The name of the beast is an Islamic name;

- The mark of the beast is the Ash Shahadatan (the display of the Arabic symbols that declare that "there is no god but Allah and Muhammad is his prophet");

- The number of the beast is not a number, but is that which identifies the multitude of his name (the name of the beast), which is "in the name of Allah".

- The image of the beast:

- How to wear it on your forehead:

Traitor to U.S.
& to
God!

CHAPTER FIFTEEN

The Beast Rising Up Out of the Sea

We begin with the words of Christ in the gospel of Matthew, which has sparked eschatological inquiry from the moment he said it through to the present.

> "Therefore when you see the *'abomination of desolation,* spoken of by Daniel the prophet, standing in the holy place" (whoever reads, let him understand), "then let those who are in Judea flee to the mountains. Let him who is on the housetop not go down to take anything out of his house. And let him who is in the field not go back to get his clothes. But woe to those who are pregnant and to those who are nursing babies in those days! And pray that your flight may not be in winter or on the Sabbath. For then there will be great tribulation, such as has not been since the beginning of the world until this time, no, nor ever shall be. And unless those days were

shortened, no flesh would be saved; but for the elect's sake those days will be shortened." Matthew 24:15-22.

There are two criteria that establish the time when Judea faces "great tribulation, such as has not been since the beginning of the world until this time, no, nor ever shall be": when you see the abomination of desolation, and when you see it standing in the holy place.

Let's see if we can establish what is the abomination of desolation.

> "And from the time *that* the daily *sacrifice* is taken away, and the abomination of desolation is set up, *there shall be* one thousand two hundred and ninety days. Blessed *is* he who waits, and comes to the one thousand three hundred and thirty-five days. "But you, go *your way* till the end; for you shall rest, and will arise

to your inheritance at the end of the days." Daniel 12:11-13.

These *are* the people whom Nebuchadnezzar carried away captive: in the seventh year, three thousand and twenty-three Jews; in the eighteenth year of Nebuchadnezzar he carried away captive from Jerusalem eight hundred and thirty-two persons; in the twenty-third year of Nebuchadnezzar, Nebuzaradan the captain of the guard carried away captive of the Jews seven hundred and forty-five persons. All the persons *were* four thousand six hundred. Jeremiah 52:28-30.

Jehoiakim took the throne at the age of twenty-five, 2 Kings 23.36, and reigned for eleven years between 609 and 598 BC. The captivity began then in 606 BC and ended three years following the edict of Cyrus the Great in 539 BC. The twenty-third year of the reign of Nebuchadnezzar would then be 584

BC (counting 606 BC as year '1'). This last removal of Jews from Judea was the last year of the practice of sacrifice, and the people and the sacrifice were "taken away" – not just merely "ended."

> "And from the time *that* the daily *sacrifice* is taken away, and the abomination of desolation is set up, *there shall be* one thousand two hundred and ninety days."

Once again, we must calculate the 1,290 days as 1,290 years, given the edict found in Ezekiel.

> "Lie also on your left side, and lay the iniquity of the house of Israel upon it. *According* to the number of the days that you lie on it, you shall bear their iniquity. For I have laid on you the years of their iniquity, according to the number of the days, three hundred and ninety days; so you shall bear the iniquity of the house of Israel. And when you have completed

them, lie again on your right side; then you shall bear the iniquity of the house of Judah forty days. I have laid on you a day for each year. Ezekiel 4:4-6.

Further, as explained above using a conversion from a lunar calendar to a solar calendar, 1,290 must be modified by a factor of .9863 (the adjustment from a 360 day year to a 365 day year), yielding 1,272 years from 584 BC, bringing us to the year 688 AD, a significant year indeed. If we apply our same measuring stick to the 1,335 days that concludes the prophecy ("Blessed *is* he who waits, and comes to the one thousand three hundred and thirty-five days") we can determine another important date.

Adjusting the 1,335 years for a solar calendar using a factor of .9863, we arrive at the year 732 AD. So here are our dates: 688

AD for the year of the set up of the abomination of desolation, and 732 for the blessing for those who wait.

2. 688 AD:

Built atop the earlier location of the Temple, the Dome of the Rock, Also known as Kubbat as-Sakhra, Kubbet es Sakhra, "Mosque of Omar," Qubbet el-Sakhra, Templum Domini, was erected by the Muslim ruler Abd el-Malik in 688-691.[25]

732 AD:

October 10, 732 AD marks the conclusion of the Battle of Tours, arguably one of the most decisive battles in all of history.
A Moslem army, in a crusading search for land and the end of Christianity, after the conquest of Syria, Egypt, and North Africa, began to invade Western Europe under the leadership of Abd-er

---

[25] BiblePlaces.com
http://www.bibleplaces.com/domeofrock.htm

Rahman, governor of Spain. Abd-er Rahman led an infantry of 60,000 to 400,000 soldiers across the Western Pyrenees and toward the Loire River, but they were met just outside the city of Tours by Charles Martel, known as the Hammer, and the Frankish Army.

Martel gathered his forces directly in the path of the oncoming Moslem army and prepared to defend themselves by using a phalanx style of combat. The invading Moslems rushed forward, relying on the slashing tactics and overwhelming number of horsemen that had brought them victories in the past. However, the French Army, composed of foot soldiers armed only with swords, shields, axes, javelins, and daggers, was well trained. Despite the effectiveness of the Moslem army in previous battles, the terrain caused them a disadvantage. Their strength lied within their cavalry, armed with large swords and lances, which along with their baggage mules, limited their mobility.

The French army displayed great ardency in withstanding the ferocious attack. It was one of the rare times in the Middle Ages when infantry held its ground against a mounted attack. The exact length of the battle is undetermined; Arab sources claim that it was a two day battle whereas Christian sources hold that the fighting clamored on for seven days. In either case, the battle ended when the French captured and killed Abd-er Rahman. The Moslem army withdrew peacefully overnight and even though Martel expected a surprise retaliation, there was none. For the Moslems, the death of their leader caused a sharp setback and they had no choice but to retreat back across the Pyrenees, never to return again.

Not only did this prove to be an extremely decisive battle for the Christians, but the Battle of Tours is considered the high water mark of the Moslem invasion of Western Europe.[26]

Let us then see if these dates have any application in modern prophecy.

> And there appeared a great wonder in heaven; a woman clothed with the sun, and the moon under her feet, and upon her head *a crown of twelve stars*: And she being with child cried, travailing in birth, and pained to be delivered. And there appeared another wonder in heaven; and behold a great red dragon, having seven heads and ten horns, and seven crowns upon his heads. And his tail drew the third part of the stars of heaven, and did cast them to the earth: and the dragon stood before the woman which was ready to be delivered, for to devour her child as soon as it was born. And she brought

---

[26] The Battle of Tours, The Web Chronology Project, Western and Central Europe Chronology

http://www.thenagain.info/webchron/WestEurope/Tours.html

forth a man child, who was to rule all nations with a rod of iron: and her child was caught up unto God, and to his throne. And the woman fled into the wilderness, where she hath a place prepared of God, that they should feed her there a thousand two hundred and threescore days. Revelation 12:1-6.

This passage tells us that this woman is the tribes of Israel as she is "clothed in the sun" (the chosen people), has the moon under her feet (the lunar calendar) and has a crown of twelve stars (twelve angels, representing the 12 tribes of Israel). "She brought forth a man child, who was to rule all nations with a rod of iron (which is to say the Christ child) and her child was caught up unto God (the ascension), and to his throne. And the woman fled into the wilderness, where she hath a place prepared of God, that they should feed her there a thousand two hundred and threescore (1,260) days.

The last of the tribes of Israel (Judah, Benjamin and Levi) were scattered with the rise of Islam, particularly following the slaughter of the last remaining major tribe of Jews in Medina, the Qurayza. Once the Dome of the Rock was constructed on the Temple Mount, the Jews left the area, returning home and establishing the nation of Israel again in 1948 – 1, 260 years later.

In addition, the Dome of the Rock was constructed on an area of the Temple Mount that has since turned out to be the "outer court" of the second temple. Consider the following passage:

> But the court which is without the
> temple leave out, and measure it not;
> for it is given unto the Gentiles: and

the holy city shall they tread under foot forty-two months.

When you consider that there are 365 ¼ days in a year, and that the average month in the solar calendar is therefore 30.44 days, forty-two months then translates into 1,278 ½ years. If the trampling of the outer court began mid-year, or 688 ½ AD, and they trampled it for forty-two months, or 1, 278 ½ years, we arrive at the year 1967, the year Jerusalem was recaptured by the nation of Israel.

Given the markers, it is safe to say that the abomination of desolation is that place of worship known as the Dome of the Rock, the oldest Islamic building in the world.

Let us consider the prophecy that spells out our beast that rises out of the sea:

> And I stood upon the sand of the sea, and saw a beast rise up out of the sea, having seven heads and ten horns, and upon his horns ten crowns, and upon his heads the name of blasphemy.

We have already discussed this beast and its identity – the financial coalition between the Arabic world and the Roman world. It rises up out of the sea of humanity.

> And the beast which I saw was like unto a leopard, and his feet were as the feet of a bear, and his mouth as the mouth of a lion: and the dragon gave him his power, and his seat, and great authority. Revelation 13:2.

This description tells us of the spirit of the beast – it is like unto a leopard, its feet *as* a bear and its mouth *as* a lion. In Daniel, the leopard is described as having "dominion given to it"; the bear "devours much flesh" and the mouth of the lion is "lifted up from the earth and made to stand on two feet like a man, and a man's heart was given to it." Daniel 7:1-6.

The beast that rises from the sea is like a kingdom that has dominion given to it, it is footed in a kingdom that devours much flesh, and has a mouth like a kingdom lifted up from the earth and made to stand on two feet like a man and with a man's heart.

> And I saw one of his heads as it were wounded to death; and his deadly wound was healed: and all the world wondered after the beast. And they worshipped the dragon which gave power unto the beast: and they worshipped the beast, saying: Who is like unto the beast? who is able to make war with him?
>
> Revelation 13:3-4

This predicts that one of the seven heads of the seven-headed and ten horned beast would be as though it was wounded to death but the deadly wound has healed. To fully understand this, we must look later at Revelation 17:

> And there came one of the seven angels which had the seven vials, and talked with me, saying unto me, Come hither; I will shew unto thee the judgment of the great whore that sitteth upon many waters:
>
> With whom the kings of the earth have committed fornication, and the inhabitants of the earth have been made drunk with the wine of her fornication.

> - Revelation 17:1-2

Fornication before God is always the worship of false gods, the worship of Baal

and the worship of Asherah. The worship of
Baal began under Nimrod (Ninus), and the
worship of Asherah (Ishtar) began with the
worship of the daughter of Ninus. This
worship began in Babylon, the city first
created by Ninus. The great whore is
therefore that social order and social system
that has always worshipped Baal and
Asherah without abatement.

> [3]So he carried me away in the spirit
> into the wilderness: and I saw a
> woman sit upon a scarlet coloured
> beast, full of names of blasphemy,
> having seven heads and ten horns.
>
> -   Revelation 17:3

The woman is sitting on the beast –
the same beast that comes out of the sea in
Revelation 13 – in the "wilderness" which is

to say, not in an otherwise previously identified place.

> ⁴And the woman was arrayed in purple and scarlet colour, and decked with gold and precious stones and pearls, having a golden cup in her hand full of abominations and filthiness of her fornication:
>
> ⁵And upon her forehead was a name written, MYSTERY, BABYLON THE GREAT, THE MOTHER OF HARLOTS AND ABOMINATIONS OF THE EARTH.
>
> -   Revelation 17:4-5

The woman has a name written on her forehead which tells us of her identity: she is a mystery; she is of Babylon the Great; she is of the mother of harlots, and the mother of the abominations of the earth.

> And I saw the woman drunken with the blood of the saints, and with

the blood of the martyrs of Jesus: and when I saw her, I wondered with great admiration.

And the angel said unto me, Wherefore didst thou marvel? I will tell thee the mystery of the woman, and of the beast that carrieth her, which hath the seven heads and ten horns.

The beast that thou sawest was, and is not; and shall ascend out of the bottomless pit, and go into perdition: and they that dwell on the earth shall wonder, whose names were not written in the book of life from the foundation of the world, when they behold the beast that was, and is not, and yet is.

And here is the mind which hath wisdom. The seven heads are seven mountains, on which the woman sitteth.

And there are seven kings: five are fallen, and one is, and the other is

not yet come; and when he cometh, he
must continue a short space.

-   Revelation 17:6-10
-

The mistake that many commentators
make is to follow and track the kingdoms
ruling over Jerusalem, yet, this is a discussion
about Babylon. Let us contemplate the
kingdoms that have ruled over the land of
Shinar, the land of the Chaldeans.

1. Egyptian   [fallen]

2. Assyrian   [fallen]

3. Babylonian   [fallen]

4. Medo-Persian   [fallen]

5. Greek/Seleucid   [fallen]

6. Roman/Byzantine

    [falling at that time]

7. Ottoman   [to come]

And the beast that was, and is not, even he is the eighth, and is of the seven, and goeth into perdition.

And the ten horns which thou sawest are ten kings, which have received no kingdom as yet; but receive power as kings one hour with the beast.

These have one mind, and shall give their power and strength unto the beast.

These shall make war with the Lamb, and the Lamb shall overcome them: for he is Lord of lords, and King of kings: and they that are with him are called, and chosen, and faithful.

-   Revelation 17:11-14

This war is discussed to some detail in Ezekiel 38 – those who would make war with the Lamb. Let us consider who they are:

Behold, I am against thee, O Gog,
the chief prince of Meshech and Tubal:
-   Ezekiel 38:3

Contrary to the commentators who have insisted that Meshech and Tubal refer to Moscow and Tobolsk, Russia, these places actually refer to the historic lands of the Assyrian Empire, governed by the city of Nineveh. This is consistent with Amos's designation of Gog and the prince of the locusts who are described as the armies of Assyria in Amos 7 (Septuagint).

Persia, Sudan, and Libya are with Meshech and Tubal, Ezekiel 38:5, as are Gomer, Togarmah, Sheba, Dedan and Tarshish, which is to say, ten kings. Persia, Sudan and Libya join with the provinces of modern Turkey, Ethiopia and Eritrea to make war with the Lamb.

And he saith unto me, The waters which thou sawest, where the whore sitteth, are peoples, and multitudes, and nations, and tongues.

And the ten horns which thou sawest upon the beast, these shall hate the whore, and shall make her desolate and naked, and shall eat her flesh, and burn her with fire.

For God hath put in their hearts to fulfil his will, and to agree, and give their kingdom unto the beast, until the words of God shall be fulfilled.

And the woman which thou sawest is that great city, which reigneth over the kings of the earth.

Let us consider that the beast which rises out of the sea is not Babylonian, but *Assyrian*, while the great whore who rides the beast is the Babylonian system of worship, made manifest in the worship of Baal and the worship of Ishtar. The beast hates the great whore, whose center is the great city (Rome) who had kingdom over the kings of the land at the time of John.

The coalition of the G-7/8 and OAPEC nations (the recreated Babylon) as controlled by the Catholic white pope and the Jesuit black pope when unified with Sunni Islam to worship Baal (Allah) and Ishtar (Mary or al Uzza) under an orchestrated *New World Order* that forces this unified ecumenical religious system on the world, will be that which is destroyed by the rising *Assyrian* beast – the alliance that will look like the empire of Alexander the Great (the leopard), will have the its foundations (feet) in Persia (the bear), and will speak like Babylon (the lion).

In 1924, the remnant of the Ottoman empire collapsed, and the Caliphate, having lost its Caliph, ended, the empire having suffered a "fatal head wound." The eighth empire which is of the seven is a Shiite Islamic Assyrian empire.

> And there was given unto him a mouth speaking great things and blasphemies; and power was given unto him to continue forty and two months. And he opened his mouth in blasphemy against God, to blaspheme his name, and his tabernacle, and them that dwell in heaven. Revelation 13:5-6.

Here, the beast which rises out of the sea is given a mouth. In our earlier passage, the beast is said to have the mouth of a lion. When these passages are combined, it appears that the beast will then use this mouth of the lion to speak great things and blasphemies against God, against God's name, against his tabernacle and against those in heaven.

Daniel tell us of such a lion when his vision reveal an event when "four beasts came up from the sea."

The winged lion of Nebuchadnezzar's Babylon, with a human head and three crowns.

And four great beasts came up from the sea, diverse one from another. The *first was like a lion, and had eagle's wings*: I beheld till the wings thereof were plucked, and it was lifted up from the earth, and made stand upon the feet as a man, and a man's heart was given to it. Daniel 7:3-4.

The beast of Revelation 13 is given the power to speak blasphemies for forty-two months, and he speaks with the mouth of the lion of Babylon, the source of all things pagan, including the worship of Baal (sun) worship, Moleck (half man, half bull) worship, Dagon worship (half man, half fish) and worship of the "queen of heaven" Astarte (Asherah, Ashtoreth, Isis, Inana, Diana, Morgana, the fertility goddess worshipped throughout the world, often worshipped as mother and infant son).

To utter blasphemies against God, the beast will be empowered to assign evil to God – to blame God for the despicable condition of man; to speak against God's name, against his tabernacle and against those in heaven. Ultimately, this new beast will denounce God with all pagan enthusiasm as part of the rise of Babylonian pagan practices, which will ultimately include child sacrifice and cannibalism.

> For the wrath of God is revealed from heaven against all ungodliness and unrighteousness of men, who hold the truth in unrighteousness; Because that which may be known of God is manifest in them; for God hath shewed it unto them. For the invisible things of him from the creation of the world are clearly seen, being understood by the things that are made, even his eternal power and Godhead; so that they are without excuse:

Because that, when they knew God, they glorified him not as God, neither were thankful; but became vain in their imaginations, and their foolish heart was darkened. Professing themselves to be wise, they became fools, And changed the glory of the uncorruptible God into an image made like to corruptible man, and to birds, and four-footed beasts, and creeping things.

Wherefore God also gave them up to uncleanness through the lusts of their own hearts, to dishonour their own bodies between themselves: Who changed the truth of God into a lie, and worshipped and served the creature more than the Creator, who is blessed forever. Amen.

For this cause God gave them up unto vile affections: for even their women did change the natural use into that which is against nature: And likewise also the men, leaving the natural use of the woman, burned in their lust one toward another; men with men working that which is unseemly, and receiving in themselves that recompence of their error which was meet.

And even as they did not like to retain God in their knowledge, God gave them over to a reprobate mind, to do those things which are not convenient; Being filled with all unrighteousness, fornication, wickedness, covetousness, maliciousness; full of envy, murder, debate, deceit, malignity; whisperers, Backbiters, haters of God, despiteful, proud, boasters, inventors of evil things, disobedient to parents, Without understanding, covenant breakers, without natural affection, implacable, unmerciful: Who knowing the judgment of God, that they which commit such things are worthy of death, not only do the same, but have pleasure in them that do them.

Romans 1:18-32.

Those practices described in Romans 1 are the new morality of the order among the nations under the beast. The world of

today is replete with all of these practices.
The only thing that remains is the rise of the
beast over all those who dwell on the earth.
From these practices, the words of the ruling
class will rise to express pleasure in "them
that do them," and from these words will
arise blasphemies against God, His name, His
tabernacle and the saints.

The spirit of antichrist will be found
also in the beast. Consider that within the
Dome of the Rock mosque on the temple
mount in Jerusalem are the words "O you
People of the Book, overstep not bounds in
your religion, and of God speak only the
truth. The Messiah, Jesus, son of Mary, is only
an apostle of God, and his Word which he
conveyed unto Mary, and a Spirit proceeding
from him. Believe therefore in God and his
apostles, and say not Three. It will be better

for you. God is only one God. Far be it from His transcendent majesty that he should have a son."

> Who is a liar but he that denieth that Jesus is the Christ? He is antichrist, that denieth the Father and the Son. 23 Whosoever denieth the Son, the same hath not the Father: [(but) he that acknowledgeth the Son hath the Father also]. 1 John 2:22.

The beast therefore is found with both the spirit of Babylon, and the spirit of antichrist.

> And it was given unto him to make war with the saints, and to overcome them: and power was given him over all kindreds, and tongues, and nations. And all that dwell upon the earth shall worship him, whose names are not written in the book of life of the Lamb slain from the foundation of the world. Revelation 13:7-8.

This is pretty clear. "All that dwell upon the earth shall worship him." I do not think you can limit the scope of this statement, particularly when you consider the statement from the prior sentence that this beast would have power over all kindreds, all tongues and all nations. That pretty well sizes it up, with of course the singular exception: those whose names are "written in the book of life of the Lamb slain from the foundation of the world." There will be two groups of people on earth: those worshipping the beast which rises out of the sea, and those whose names are found in the book of life. There are no other choices.

> If any man have an ear, let him hear. He that leadeth into captivity shall go into captivity: he that killeth with the sword must be killed with the

sword. Here is the patience and the faith of the saints. Revelation 13:9-10.

Here is the last of it. Those whose names are found in the book of life are warned to be patient and to not fight the rise of the beast; and it is equally true that those who take the saints captive will also be taken captive, and those who kill with the sword, will be killed by the sword.

CHAPTER SIXTEEN

The Mahdi Criteria

In Islam, there is also an ascending
end-times figure: the Mahdi (the
reincarnation of the Twelfth Imam). The
Mahdi is a foreordained leader who will rise
to launch a great social transformation in
order to restore and adjust all things under
divine guidance. The Mahdi – an Islamic
"messiah" – will bring true and uncorrupted
guidance to all mankind, creating a just social
order and a world free from oppression in
which the Islamic revelation will be the norm
for all nations.[27]

Generally, here are the qualifications
for the Twelfth Imam, or Mahdi:

---

[27] Sachedina, Abdulaziz Abdjuljussein, *Islamic
Messianism, The Idea of the Mahdi in Twelver Shi'ism*,
Albany State University of New York, 1981.

1. The Prophet said: The Mahdi will be of my family, of the descendants of Fatimah.

Fatimah, the daughter of Muhammad, had three sons, of which two survived passed infancy: Hasan and Hussein (Husayn). Ḥusayn ibn ʿAlī ibn Abī Ṭālib was the grandson of the Islamic prophet Muhammad and the son of Ali, the first Imam, and the fourth Caliph, and Muhammad's daughter Fatima Zahra. Hussein ibn Ali is revered as a martyr who fought tyranny, as the third Imam by most Shi'a Muslims, and as the second Imam by the majority of Ismaili Shi'a Muslims.

2. The Mahdi will pave the way for and establish the government of the community of Muhammad, as the Vice-Regent to Allah, and every believer will be obligated to support him.

Then I saw another beast coming up out of the earth, and he had two horns like a lamb and spoke like a dragon. And he exercises all the authority of the first beast in his presence, and causes the earth and those who dwell in it to worship the first beast, whose deadly wound was healed. He performs great signs, so that he even makes fire come down from heaven on the earth in the sight of men. And he deceives those who dwell on the earth by those signs which he was granted to do in the sight of the beast, telling those who dwell on the earth to make an image to the beast who was wounded by the sword and lived. He was granted *power* to give breath to the image of the beast, that the image of the beast should both speak and cause as many as would not worship the image of the beast to be killed. He causes all, both small and great, rich and poor, free and slave, to receive a mark on their right hand or on their foreheads, and that no one may buy or sell except one who has the mark or the name of the beast, or the number of his name. Revelation 13:11-17.

3. The Mahdi will rule the Muslim and non-Muslim world together.

The Mahdi will fight against the forces of evil, lead a world revolution and set up a new world order based on justice, righteousness and virtue . . . ultimately the righteous will take the world administration in their hands and Islam will be victorious over all the religions.

> And he causeth all, both small and great, rich and poor, free and bond, to receive a mark in their right hand, or in their foreheads: Revelation 13:16

4. The Mahdi will engage in jihad against non-believers.

The Mahdi will receive a pledge of allegiance as a caliph for Muslims. He will lead Muslims in many battles of jihad. His reign will be a caliphate that follows the guidance of the Prophet. Many battles will ensue between Muslims and the disbelievers during the Mahdi's reign.

5. The Mahdi's ascendancy to power will follow the rise of an army from the east that will be carrying the black flags of war.

Hadith indicate that black flags coming from the area of Khorasan (Iran) will signify that the appearance of the Mahdi is nigh.

Monday, April 02, 2007

The Black Flag Flying: The Arabs and Iran ally against the West

Last week's Arab League summit in
Riyadh will be looked on by future historians
as a major turning point in the War on Jihad.
Along with the Mecca Summit and the
historic meeting between Iran's President
Ahmadinejad and Saudi King Abdullah in
Riyadh last month, it symbolized the failure

of President Bush's Middle East policy and his efforts to enlist Sunni `allies' against Shiite Iran.

The Saudis, like Iran have taken note of the composition of the new Congress, the tilt towards appeasement and the votes to undercut President Bush's role as commander in chief as well as the West's feeble response to Iran's defiance of the UN and the seizure of British hostages at sea.

The non-Arab guests of honor at Riyadh were Iranian foreign minister Manoucher Mottaki and Iranian Chief of Staff General Hassan Fayrouz Abadi , who were there to solidify the understandings between King Abdullah and Ahmadinejad at their earlier meeting.

Black flags and veils as religion returns to campuses of Iraq

By Robert Fisk in Baghdad - 29 March 2004

http://www.robert-fisk.com/articles384.htm

The black flags of Muharram
are draped over the front of the School
of Arts, banners of mourning erected
by Shias at the vast campus of the
University of Baghdad. The words
praise Imam Hussein's revolution in
the seventh century against the
Omayads and they seek to draw all
students - Christian as well as Sunni -
into their tears of martyrdom.

Iraq Flag

Jumhuriyyat al-'Iraq, The Republic of Iraq[28]

Arab Revolt Flag, Arab Liberation Flag

Last modified: **2007-05-05**

---

[28] http://www.flags.de/fotw/flags/iq.html

Last modified: 2008-01-26

The color of black: The Prophet Mohammad (570-632)

In the seventh century, with the rise of Islam and subsequent liberation of Mecca, two flags - one white, one black - were carried. On the white flag was written, "There is no god but God (Allah) and Mohammad is the Prophet of God."

The black flag was a sign of revenge. It was the color of the headdress worn when leading troops into battle. Both black and white flags were placed in the mosque during Friday prayers.

It is noteworthy that the Pan-Arab Revolt Flag and the Arab Liberation Flag have the same colors as the new Iraqi flag. In white and in Arabic is the statement "There is no god but Allah and Mohammad is his Prophet," and the color black was added to the flag this year (2008).

Let us consider the rising army in Iran. Iran maintains three armies within their territory, the Army, the Pásdárán and the Basij. The Islamic Republic of Iran Army, the Artesh, is the ground force of the Military of Islamic Republic of Iran. As of 2006, the regular Iranian Army was estimated to have

350,000 personnel (220,000 conscripts and 130,000 professionals).

The Pásdárán have their own ministry, and are thought to number as many as 120,000 with their own small naval and air units. They also control the Basij volunteer force. Currently Basij have a local organization in just about every city in Iran and serve as an auxiliary force engaged in activities such as law enforcement, emergency management, social service providing, public religious ceremony organizing, and more controversially morals policing and dissident gathering suppressing.

6. The Mahdi will be victorious over and eradicate the Israelis, by abolishing their leadership and establishing Jerusalem as the center of Islamic rule – the Caliphate.

And Jesus went out, and
departed from the temple: and his

disciples came to him for to shew him the buildings of the temple. And Jesus said unto them, See ye not all these things? verily I say unto you, There shall not be left here one stone upon another, that shall not be thrown down.

And as he sat upon the mount of Olives, the disciples came unto him privately, saying, Tell us, when shall these things be? and what shall be the sign of thy coming, *and of the end of the world*?

And Jesus answered and said unto them, Take heed that no man deceive you. For many shall come in my name, saying, I am Christ; and shall deceive many. And ye shall hear of wars and rumours of wars: see that ye be not troubled: for all these things must come to pass, but the end is not yet. For nation shall rise against nation, and kingdom against kingdom: and there shall be famines, and pestilences, and earthquakes, in divers places. All these are the beginning of sorrows.

Then shall they deliver you up to be afflicted, and shall kill you: and ye shall be hated of all nations for my name's sake. And then shall many be offended, and shall betray one another, and shall hate one another. And many false prophets shall rise, and shall deceive many. And because iniquity shall abound, the love of many shall wax cold. But he that shall endure unto the end, the same shall be saved.

And this gospel of the kingdom shall be preached in all the world for a witness unto all nations; and then shall the end come. When ye therefore shall see the abomination of desolation, spoken of by Daniel the prophet, stand in the holy place, (whoso readeth, let him understand:)

Then let them which be in Judaea flee into the mountains: Let him which is on the housetop not come down to take anything out of his house: Neither let him which is in the field return back to take his clothes. And woe unto them that are with child, and to them that give suck in those days! But pray ye that your flight be not in the winter, neither on the sabbath day: For then shall be great tribulation, such as was not since the beginning of the world to this time, no, nor ever shall be. And except those days should be shortened, there should no flesh be saved: but for the elect's sake those days shall be shortened.

Then if any man shall say unto you, Lo, here is Christ, or there; believe it not. For there shall arise false Christs, and false prophets, and shall shew great signs and wonders; insomuch that, if it were possible, they shall deceive the very elect. Behold, I have told you before. Wherefore if they shall say unto you, Behold, he is in the desert; go not forth: behold, he is in the secret chambers; believe it not. For as the lightning cometh out of the east, and shineth even unto the west; so shall also the coming of the Son of man be. For wheresoever the carcase is, there will the eagles be gathered together.

Immediately after the tribulation of those days shall the sun be darkened, and the moon shall not give her light, and the stars shall fall from heaven, and the powers of the heavens shall be shaken: And then shall appear the sign of the Son of man in heaven: and then shall all the tribes of the earth mourn, and they shall see the Son of man coming in the clouds of heaven with power and great glory. And he shall send his angels with a great sound of a trumpet, and they shall gather together his elect from the four winds, from one end of heaven to the other.

Now learn a parable of the fig tree; When his branch is yet tender, and putteth forth leaves, ye know that summer is nigh: So likewise ye, when ye shall see all these things, know that it is near, even at the doors. Verily I say unto you, This generation shall not pass, till all these things be fulfilled. Heaven and earth shall pass away, but my words shall not pass away.

But of that day and hour knoweth no man, no, not the angels of heaven, but my Father only. But as the days of Noah were, so shall also the coming of the Son of man be. For as in the days that were before the flood they were eating and drinking, marrying and giving in marriage, until the day that Noah entered into the ark, And knew not until the flood came, and took them all away; so shall also the coming of the Son of man be. Then shall two be in the field; the one shall be taken, and the other left. Two women shall be grinding at the mill; the one shall be taken, and the other left. Watch therefore: for ye know not what hour your Lord doth come.

But know this, that if the goodman of the house had known in what watch the thief would come, he would have watched, and would not have suffered his house to be broken up. Therefore be ye also ready: for in such an hour as ye think not the Son of man cometh.

Matthew 24:1-43.

8. The Mahdi will be a miraculous provider who will be loved by all.

The coming of the *lawless one* is according to the working of Satan, with all power, signs, and lying wonders, and with all unrighteous deception among those who perish, because they did not receive the love of the truth, that they might be saved. And for this reason God will send them strong delusion, that they should believe the lie, that they all may be condemned who did not believe the truth but had pleasure in unrighteousness. 2Thess. 2: 9-12.

He performs great signs, so that he even makes fire come down from heaven on the earth in the sight of men. And he deceives those who dwell on the earth by those signs which he was granted to do in the sight of the beast, telling those who dwell on the earth to make an image to the beast who was wounded by the sword and lived. Revelation 13:13-14.

8. The Mahdi will come to power immediately following a peace treaty brokered by a Jew from the priesthood of Aaron between the Arabs and the "Romans," (now, the modern EU, or the West) and will be upheld for seven years.

There are two things to consider in this prophecy: first that a peace treaty will be brokered between the Arabs and the Romans – a treaty before that has been shown to create the beast that rises from the sea. (See preceding chapter); second, the length of this deal is only for seven years, which should it begin in 2009 would coincide with Daniel's last seven weeks (weeks 63-69) where each week is considered a year.

9. The Mahdi will reign for seven years, dividing property, governing by the Sunnah, and filling the earth with equity and justice, then he will die, and be mourned by Muslims.

Once again, we have an indication that these events will take place is the last seven weeks of Daniel's seventy weeks, and this prophecy is consistent with the prophecy in Revelation 13 indicating that the beast which rises from earth will cause all those who dwell on the earth to worship the beast (Islam) to accept his mark (Sharia) or his number (the Quran).

10. The Mahdi will ride the white horse and judge by the Qur'an, and with men who will have marks of prostration on their foreheads (from bowing in prayer five times daily).

Now I saw when the Lamb opened one of the seals; and I heard one of the four living creatures saying with a voice like thunder, "Come and see." And I looked, and behold, a white horse. He who sat on it had a bow; and a crown was given to him, and he went out conquering and to conquer. Revelation 6:1-2.

Of the twenty-one events set forth in the prophecy of the book of Revelation (the seven seals, the seven trumpets, and the seven bowls of wrath), the very first is the arrival of a white horse. This white horse is known in Islamic eschatology as well.

An animal by the name of *Buraq,* apparently horse-like and white, and with a human face, was provided for a ride from the mosque in Mecca to the al-Aqsa mosque in Jerusalem, from where he ascended, supposedly on a ladder of light to the seven heavens.

The story of the Ascension of Mohammed, known as "Miraj", or "Stairway to Heaven" began when Mohammed fell asleep on a carpet at his cousin's place and became the inspirational source of different "Stories of the 1001 Nights of Arabia" involving "Magic Carpet Rides". The following is a resume of this fabulous dream....

"Mohammad had gone to rest at dusk. He slept deeply on the carpet of his cousin, Mutem ibn Adi. Suddenly, the silence was broken and a voice as clear as a trumpet called :

"Awake, thou sleeper, awake!" And Mohammed saw in front of him, dazzling in darkness the shining Archangel Gabriel who was inviting him to follow him outside. Before the door stood a Horse as dazzling as Gabriel. It had wings, glittering wings of an immense eagle. Gabriel presented the Horse to Mohammed, saying that it was "*Burak*" the Horse of Abraham. *Burak* whinnied and allowed Mohammed to vault on its back.

Then, drinking the wind, it galloped to the street and as it came to the walls of the sleeping city, it spread its wings and soared into the starry night.

First of all, they went to the summit of Mount Sinai, at the very place where Jehovah had given the stone tables to Moses. Then, they flew on and went to Bethlehem at the exact place where Jesus was born. And finally, depending on the different versions, they went to Heaven, or into a Holy Temple in Heaven.

11. The Mahdi will discover and bring out the Torah and the Gospel from a town called Antioch.

Antakya (Arabic: اناطاك ية, Greek: Ἀντιόχεια Antiókheia or Antiócheia) is the seat of the Hatay Province in southern Turkey, near the border with Syria. In ancient times the city was known as Antioch and has historical significance for Christianity, being the place where the followers of Jesus Christ were called Christians for the very first time. The city and its massive walls also played an important role during the Crusades.

12. The Mahdi will rediscover the Ark of the Covenant, which he will bring to Jerusalem.

It is interesting that in Islamic prophecy, the Mahdi recovers the Ark of the Covenant. This is consistent with the Surah *The Cow*, where the Torah and the Gospel are declared to be true.

13. The Mahdi will have supernatural power over the wind, the rain and crops.

Even him, whose coming is after the working of Satan with all power and signs and lying wonders, 2 Thess. 2:9.

He performs great signs, so that he even makes fire come down from heaven on the earth in the sight of men. And he deceives those who dwell on the earth by those signs which he was granted to do in the sight of the beast, telling those who dwell on the earth to make an image to the beast who was wounded by the sword and lived. Revelation 13:13-14.

14. The Mahdi will have enormous amounts of wealth.

But, of course. Consider the following:

Ongoing $134.5 Billion Bearer Bond Mystery: Possible Link to Upcoming Bank Holiday

by: J. S. Kim July 16, 2009
http://seekingalpha.com/article/149213-ongoing-134-5-billion-bearer-bond-mystery-possible-link-to-upcoming-bank-holiday

PART THREE:

THE ACTIONS OF THE MAN OF LAWLESSNESS

Chapter Seventeen

The occultism of Barack Hussein Obama

> And to the angel of the church in Pergamos write; These things saith he which hath the sharp sword with two edges;
>
> I know thy works, and where thou dwellest, *even where Satan's throne is*: and thou holdest fast my name, and hast not denied my faith, even in those days wherein Antipas was my faithful martyr, who was slain among you, *where Satan dwelleth.*
>
> - Revelation 2:12-13

Pergamos (also Pergamum or Pergamon) is an interesting place. The remains of the original acropolis are quite significant, as the outcropping rises steeply against the plain of modern Bergama, Turkey. It is worth the time to look at this site Google Earth. You will discover that the site is marked by a gigantic sickle moon and star in the earth, easily visible from 25,000 feet.

Consider again the passage in Isaiah 14:

"How you are fallen from heaven, O Day Star, son of Dawn!
How you are cut down to the ground, you who laid the nations low!
You said in your heart, 'I will ascend to heaven; above the stars of God. I will set my throne on high; I will sit on the mount of assembly in the far reaches of the north;
I will ascend above the heights of the clouds; I will make myself like the Most High.'
-Isaiah 14:12-14 (ESB)

The "day star, son of Dawn" has been interpreted by many bible scholars as Lucifer, son of the morning (KJV). Lucifer is a later term meaning light bearer. In either event, the symbol of the "day star" is a star centered within a sickle moon, the insignia of Satan.

(Compare with the single star over Bethlehem, for instance). The declaration of Jesus in the book of Revelation tells us that a star is actually an angel:

> As for the mystery of the seven stars that you saw in my right hand, and the seven golden lampstands, the seven stars are the angels of the seven churches, and the seven lampstands are the seven churches.
>
> - Revelation 1:20

This declaration that the mystery of the stars is that the stars are angels deciphers this passage in Isaiah 14, telling us that this day star is in fact an angel. This is confirmed in the book of Job, which discusses those angels who would later fall.

> "Where were you when I laid the foundation of the earth? Tell me, if you have understanding.
> Who determined its measurements— surely you know! Or who stretched the

line upon it?

On what were its bases sunk, or who laid its cornerstone, when the morning stars sang together and all the sons of God shouted for joy?

- Job 38:4-7

Let us now consider the throne or seat of Satan as it existed in the city of Pergamum. This throne was in existence in Pergamum at the time of John's Revelation. An Altar to Zeus had been constructed on the acropolis overlooking the plain. This altar was compromised and dedicated to the exaltation of Caesar Augustus as he declared himself emperor of the known world and a god. This Pergamum (or Pergamon) Altar is still in existence in most of its original form.

Consider:

The Pergamum Altar is a columned temple with stairs that lead to a platform where an eighty foot statue of Zeus was once revered. The statue is long gone, because it was removed by Caesar Augustus to proclaim himself a God that the temple might be used to revere him.

One interesting feature of the temple is the statuary around its base telling the tale of the fall of the titans or giants. This tale is told not only in Greek mythology, but it also appears in the book of Enoch. The titans/giants are referenced in the book of Genesis as well, referred to as the Nephelim.

> The Nephilim were on the earth in those days—and also afterward—when the sons of God went to the daughters of men and had children by them. They were the heroes of old, men of renown.
>
> - Genesis 6:4

If you consider the combination of Job, Revelation and Isaiah, the sons of God were in heaven witnessing the creation itself. The book of Enoch (a non-canonical book in most texts) tells us that a group of angels did rebel against God and went to the daughters of men and had children by them. These giants were eventually destroyed by God.

The Pergamum Altar dedicates its statuary to the depiction (the tragic depiction?) of the loss of the titans – the destruction of the sons of Satan and the fallen angels. There should be no doubt that the Pergamum Altar is Satan's throne, as it was known in the times of the apostle John.

This is the original site of the Pergamum Altar in the acropolis in Pergamos, Turkey. The Pergamum Altar sat at this site from the date of its construction in the second century B.C. until it was deconstructed and moved to a museum in

Berlin, Germany. The move was complete in 1897.

This altar was considered by Adolf Hitler to be an occult symbol capable of bestowing power – the power and authority of Satan – upon those whose destiny included ruling the entire world. This is strictly a spiritual understanding.

It is believed that the Pergamum Altar was constructed sometime between 175 and 160 B.C. It's construction then coincides with many events which would eventually lead to the rise of Caesar Augustus. The defeat of Babylon by Cyrus the Great led to the merger of the Babylonian state with the Medo-Persian Empire. Babylonian practices, including the worship of the moon god "Sin", the worship of the pagan goddess of fertility (the "Queen of Heaven") "Ishtar", the worship of the sun god "Baal", and the worship of the fish god "Dagon" all continued even though the gardens and the walls of Babylon had been abandoned and the city left to disintegrate.

Alexander's capture of the Medo-Persian Empire and its division into four empires did little to change the pagan practices of the east. The transition within the Seleucid Empire, however, as a result of the rise of the Parthians, caused the movement of pagan practices to migrate toward Greece.

As Athens began to wane, Rome, Carthage and Pergamos became rivals to determine who would dominate in the Mediteranean. When Antiochus IV Epiphenes – the son of sin who had desecrated the temple in Jerusalem by erecting a statue of

Jupiter in the Holiest of Holies and slaughtering a pig on the temple altar – was defeated in repeated battles with Judas Macabeaus, the world began to change with significance.

Pergamos then adopted all of the pagan practices of Babylon, and sought to compete directly with Athens in architecture and sculpture. Part of this push included the construction of the Pergamum Altar. However, once Roman established an alliance with Simon Macabeaus, King of Judah, Rome began to emerge as the dominant power in the Mediteranean region. Pergamos immediately yielded to the authority of the Romans, and the pagan practices of Pergamos as transplanted from Babylon, were then transplanted to Rome, where many of them are practiced even today.

Between 1880 and 1897, the Germans began the process of moving the Pergamum Altar from Pergamos to Berlin. It is of some interest that the most intellectually developed, culturally astute nation on earth would then begin its transformation into what would emerge as the Nazi Third Reich.

It is of some significance that science in Germany at that time was overtaken by the writings of Ernst Haeckel, who premised all of his post 1880s theses on the notion that *ontology recapitulates phylogeny*. What did he mean with this bit of hyperbole? Consider his own statement made in 1914:

> The Caucasian, or Mediterranean man (*Homo Mediterraneus*), has from time immemorial been placed at the head of all the races of men, as the most highly developed and perfect. It is generally called the Caucasian race,

but as, among all the varieties of the species, the Caucasian branch is the least important, we prefer the much more suitable appellation proposed by Friedrich Müller, namely, that of *Mediterranese.* For the most important varieties of this species, which are moreover the most eminent actors in what is called "Universal History," first rose to a flourishing condition on the shores of the Mediterranean.... This species alone (with the exception of the Mongolian) has had an actual history; it alone has attained to that degree of civilization which seems to raise men above the rest of nature.[29]

The sequence of events is as follows: the Pergamum Altar is transported to Germany; racist evolution as developed by Charles Darwin and Ernst Haeckel becomes the dominant science in Germany; Germany

---

[29] Ernst Heackel, *The History of Creation*, 6th edition (1914), volume 2, page 429.

enters into a series of wars with its neighbors, culminating in the Holocaust which found the Germans executing millions of her neighbors as racial inferiors.

How did the Pergamum Altar fare during all of this? In 1934, on Hitler's direction, Nazi architect Albert Speer used the Pergamum Altar as the model for the Zeppelin tribune, the Nazi temple where Hitler would exalt himself as a god whose destiny was to rule the world. It is easy to recall all of those soldiers standing in the Zeppelin tribune under the huge swastikas, with Hitler bellowing his self-aggrandizing, megalomaniacal speeches urging Germans on to the ultimate destruction of their history, their culture, their arts, their way of life, their cities, their nation, their legacy and their neighbors. As a special note, the swastika is also a symbol of paganism – the mark of Ishtar, the pagan goddess of fertility.

Now that we know the background, let us consider the Democratic National Committee convention in the city of Denver in August, 2008. There are several interesting things about Denver, particularly the Denver International Airport. For instance, the horse that appears on the cover of this text is a 32' foot tall sculpture that is placed in front of the DIA. This sculpture killed the sculptor who crafted it, and it has been named the demon horse from hell. People who have seen the horse cannot seem to understand the artistic meaning of placing a red-eyed horse from hell in front of the airport. Other people believe that the layout of the runways is a depiction of the swastika.

Obama, however, decided to accept the nomination while standing on a recreation of a certain Greek-like temple, seen below:

This temple meets all of the theogony of the original Pergamum Altar, especially the central portion of the elevated platform, which was reserved for the descendants of Nyx, the primordial goddess of the night. According to Hesiod's Theogony, Nyx was

born of Chaos, and her offspring include
Aether (the spirit of Atmosphere), Hemera
(the spirit of day), Momus (blame), Ponos
(toil), Moros (fate), Thanatos (death), Hypnos
(sleep), Charon (the ferryman of Hades),
Oneiroi (dreams), Nemesis (retribution),
Apate (deception), Philotes (friendship),
Geras (age) and Eris (strife).

It is from this platform that Obama
accepted the nomination of his party to run
for the Presidency of the United States on
behalf of the Democratic Party. Here is a
picture of Barack Hussein Obama accepting
the nomination of his party on the Nyx
elevated section of his mock-up of the
Pergamum Altar, under the white horse
named Thunder.

CHAPTER EIGHTEEN

The lawless origin of Barack Hussein Obama

Stanley Ann Dunham graduated high school on Mercer Island in the spring of 1960 and finally entered the University of Hawaii on September 21, 1960. At 17 years old, she was pregnant with Barack Hussein Obama II the morning after Halloween. She married Barack Hussein Obama (Sr.) in February, 1961 at some civil ceremony on the Island of Maui.

The marriage of Stanley Ann Dunham and Barack Hussein Obama was lawless in every respect. First, to be lawfully married in Hawaii, both parties needed to be residents of Hawaii for two years before getting married. Stanley Ann Dunham had only been a resident for five months. She must have lied to get the wedding license.

Barack Hussein Obama, in the meantime, was committing bigamy, which was a crime in Hawaii at that time. Of course, who could prove it, since his first wife (and first child) was back in Kenya or Zanzibar.

In Kenya or its colony Zanzibar, polygamy was legal if you were a practicing Muslim. Barack senior's father was a convert to Islam the generation before, and Barack senior had obtained an Arabic name by the will of his converted father. Barack Hussein Obama then returned the favor by converting from Islam to atheism as a Marxist communist. By the time he married 17 year old Stanley Ann Dunham, he had repudiated his status as a Muslim, therefore losing his legal right to engage in polygamy in Kenya or

Zanzibar. (He was never forthcoming on this issue, as he married two more times while retaining his marriage to his first wife Kezia, never bothering to inform Kenyan authorities that he was no longer a Muslim). Barack senior's marriage to Stanley Ann Dunham was therefore unlawful in both Hawaii and Kenya.

Nonetheless, Barack Hussein Obama (sr.) appears to be the father of the child, in which case his citizenship automatically passes to the child. The question is: what was his citizenship? Both Kenya and Zanzibar were colonies of Great Britain in the year 1961. Residents of Kenya and Zanzibar were therefore citizens of the crown at birth.

Under the British Nationality Act of 1948, Barack Hussein Obama II was a British Citizen at birth, no matter where he was born. He has since terminated this citizenship by his failure to readopt it after being adopted by his stepfather Lolo Soetoro, who made him an Indonesian citizen.

Barack Hussein Obama II has never established by any means that he is in fact an American citizen or a natural born American citizen as required under Article II, section I of the United States Constitution, which provides as follows:

>"No Person except a natural born citizen, or a citizen of the United States at the time of the adoption of this constitution, shall be eligible to the Office of President"

To establish his being "a natural born citizen," the candidate must produce a Certificate of Live Birth from one of the fifty states of the United States. A Certification of

Live Birth is not the equivalent and is insufficient to establish live birth in the US, since the birth date and the location of the birth can be attested to by a single person without witnesses. Obama has not produced any such Certificate of Live Birth from any one of the fifty states.

To establish that he was lawfully an American citizen, Obama needed to either prove that he was born in the United States – which he has not – or prove that he was born to American parents, and to then take an oath of allegiance shortly after his 18th birthday. There is no oath of allegiance or record of taking any oath of allegiance. See *ELG v. Perkins,* 307 U.S. 325, 59 S.Ct. 884, 83 L.Ed. 1320 (1939).

In the event that Obama was born outside of the fifty United States, and when only one parent is American and the other a foreign national, the law governing his citizenship was established by the Nationality Act of 1940, Section 201, 54 Stat. 1137, [30] and

---

[30] "Section 201. The following shall be nationals and citizens of the United States at birth:

"(g) A person born outside the United States and its outlying possessions of parents one of whom is a citizen of the United States who, prior to the birth of such person, has had *ten years' residence in the United States or one of its outlying possessions, at least five of which were after attaining the age of sixteen years*, [emphasis added] the other being an alien: <u>Provided</u>, That in order to retain such citizenship, the child must reside in the United States or its outlying possessions for a period or periods totaling five years between the ages of thirteen and twenty-one years: <u>Provided further</u>, That, if the child has not taken up a residence in the United States or its outlying possessions by the time he reaches the age of sixteen years, or if he resides abroad for such a time that it becomes impossible for him to complete the five years' residence in the United States or its outlying possessions before reaching the age of twenty-one years, his American citizenship shall thereupon cease.

(h) The foregoing provisions of subsection (g) concerning retention of citizenship shall apply to a

the Immigration and Nationality Act of
1952.[31] Section 301(a)(7) of the Immigration

---

child born abroad subsequent to May 24, 1934."

[31] The Immigration and Nationality Act of June 27, 1952, 66 Stat. 163, 235, 8 U.S. Code Section 1401 (b). (Section 301 of the Act).

"Section 301. (a) The following shall be nationals and citizens of the United States at birth:

"(1) a person born in the United States, and subject to the jurisdiction thereof;

"(7) a person born outside the geographical limits of the United States and its outlying possessions of parents one of whom is an alien, and the other a citizen of the United States, who prior to the birth of such person, was physically present in the United States or its outlying possessions for a period or periods totaling not less than ten years, at least five of which were after attaining the age of fourteen years.

(b) Any person who is a national and citizen of the United States at birth under paragraph (7) of subsection (a), shall lose his nationality and citizenship unless he shall come to the United States prior to attaining the age of twenty-three years and shall immediately following any such coming be continuously physically present in the United State(s) and Nationality Act of June 27, 1952, 66 Stat. 163, 235, 8 U.S.C. §1401(b), Matter of S-F-and G-, 2 I & N Dec. 182 (B.I.A.) approved (Att'y Gen. 1944), required that when a child is born abroad and one parent is a U.S. citizen, that parent would have had to live ten (10) years in the United States, five (5) of which were after the age of fourteen. At the time of

---

for at least five years: Provided, That such physical presence follows the attainment of the age of fourteen years and precedes the age of twenty-eight years.

(c) Subsection (b) shall apply to a person born abroad subsequent to May 24, 1934: Provided, however, That nothing contained in this subsection shall be construed to alter or affect the citizenship of any person born abroad subsequent to May 24, 1934, who, prior to the effective date of this Act, has taken up a residence in the United States before attaining the age of sixteen years, and thereafter, whether before or after the effective date of this Act, complies or shall comply with the residence requirements for retention of citizenship specified in subsections (g) and (h) of section 201 of the Nationality Act of 1940, as amended."

Obama's birth, his mother was only eighteen years old, and therefore did not and could not meet the residency requirements to pass to her son U.S. Citizenship. The Act of November 6, 1966 (80 Stat. 1322), amended Section 301 (a) (7) of the Immigration and Nationality Act of 1952 to read as follows:

"Section 301 (a) (7) a person born outside the geographical limits of the United States and its outlying possessions of parents one of whom is an alien, and the other a citizen of the United States who, prior to the birth of such person, was physically present in the United States or its outlying possessions for a period or periods totaling not less than ten years, at least five of which were after attaining the age of fourteen years."

The immigration laws in effect at the time of and as amended five years after Obama's birth simply did not allow for citizenship at birth for children born abroad to a U.S. citizen parent and a non-citizen parent if the citizen parent was under the age of nineteen.

Obama has failed to demonstrate that he was born in Hawaii, and he has spent over $1.7 million to prevent people from accessing any records in Hawaii. He was born out of wedlock to an underage mother and a bigamist father who then promptly abandoned him and his mother.

In March of 1964, Anna Obama secured a non-contested divorce from Barack Obama in Hawaii, having completed the fall semester of 1961, the spring semester of 1962 and the fall semester of 1962 at the

University of Washington, while living on Capitol Hill in Seattle before returning to Hawaii. Unfortunately, Hawaii requires four years of residency for a person to obtain a divorce in Hawaii, and Anna Obama had only one year. The divorce was therefore unlawful.

Let us continue. Anna Obama then went on to marry Lolo Soetoro, and moved to Indonesia, where he apparently adopted Barack Hussein Obama, changing his name to Barry Soetoro, and making him an Indonesian citizen. Since Anna Obama was not lawfully divorced, she could not have been lawfully married to Lolo Soetoro, so the adoption was probably unlawful as well.

However, the change in citizenship and the name change were fixed as a matter of law. Barry Soetoro was no longer a citizen of Great Britain or Kenya, or the United States (if he was at all at that time). Barry Soetoro was, as a matter of law, an Indonesian Muslim.

When Barry Soetoro returned to Hawaii to live with his grandmother, he unlawfully readopted portions of his birth name, calling himself Barry Obama. He then went on to abandon his Indonesian citizenship and to deny his Muslim faith (at least until he admitted it again in 2008 to George Stephanopoulos).

Barack Obama is the name Barry Soetoro took when he ran for president, but Barack Hussein Obama is the name he took to assume office, although his birth name is allegedly Barack Hussein Obama II and his legal name is Barry Soetoro.

The president is without any lawful citizenship, without a lawful birth, without a lawful ancestry, without a lawful faith, and is holding the office of President under an assumed name. He is truly the lawless one.

CHAPTER NINETEEN

The lawless agenda of Barack Hussein Obama

The agenda of Barack Hussein Obama appears to be that of a Muslim jihadist engaged to accomplish the following three objectives: 1) Cripple the economy of the United States, and consequently the economies of the trilateral financial world; 2) Empower and authorize Turkey to re-establish the Ottoman Empire; and 3) Secure Jerusalem from the Israelis.

George Soros sycophant and New World Order play-along Barack Obama is letting the New World Order family down in a big way, yet the family hasn't yet discovered the depth of the betrayal. The European leaders paying homage to Queen Elizabeth of the UK, Queen Beatrice of the Netherlands, the central banking royalty of the house of Rothschild and the lesser house of Rockefeller, together with chief operative Giorgi Schwartz, aka George Soros do not yet recognize that the new world order that Hussein Obama is creating is one that excludes Europe under European leadership.

Barack Obama's new world order is centered on the recreation of the Ottoman Empire, to the exclusion of his handlers and their money. This is why he kissed the ring of the Saudi King. This is why his first phone call was to Abbas at the Palestinian Authority. This is why he has excused the bombers of the USS Cole, why he seeks to try KSM in a US courtroom rather than a military tribunal, and why he has been negotiating in a big way with Recep Tayyip Erdogan of Turkey.

Obama's lies are so egregious, that US Congressman Representative Joe Wilson finally had to blurt out "you lie" in the halls of Congress as a visceral response to the plethora of in-your-face misrepresentations by the prevaricator in chief during an address to the joint houses on socialized healthcare. Yet, his lies are excusable, once it is recognized that he is a Muslim furthering jihad against the West. Once this is understood, the motives of Obama become clear.

Muslims are permitted to lie about anything and everything in the furtherance of jihad, including whether or not they are Muslim. Obama tried to pretend he was Christian for a while, but even George Stephanopoulos couldn't completely cover up

Obama's admission when he referenced "my Muslim faith."

The New World Order may have had its plans for a Trans-European Community ("TEC") which would join the European Union ("EU") with the North American Union ("NAU") into a New World Order of friendly socialism and gentle genocide, but such plans are not the plans of the gentleman people used to refer to as "the one." No, his plans are completely different, and the trilateral commission would do well to pay attention to what is going on while there is still time remaining.

Crippling the economy of the United States

On objective number one: How's he doing? The only restraint this fellow has on federal spending is ink and paper. He has driven the deficit to unsustainable limits, exhausting all sources of credit and forcing the Federal Reserve to buy its own debt. *What??* Even Federal Reserve Chairman Ben Bernanke admitted that an audit of the FR could result in the collapse of the dollar because of the fraudulent internal workings of the promissory note system in worldwide application. We now suffer from depression-level unemployment, collapsing economies of scale and a GDP that has fallen by one-third since January, 2008.

Obama's solution? Spend another $3 trillion a year on socialized medicine, seize the financial industry, seize the automobile industry, seize the health care industry, and gut manufacturing and industry through the implementation of the fraudulent "cap and trade" taxation scheme.

Obama's practice of Mugabean economics has allowed the federal government to spend all of the wealth we have and all of the wealth we ever will have, and he did so in less than six months from his inauguration. Now, he wants to spend trillions more in order to further the entitlements of his cronies at the expense of national sovereignty.

However, for those who think he is working to redistribute wealth from the haves to the have-less, consider that he is simply working to completely destroy America's economy and its economic future, and he expects to take Western Europe and the ASEAN economies with us. This is *intentional destruction,* because the Ottoman Empire cannot rise to the world's only superpower if the United States remains healthy. Obama is the *agent provocateur* of Islamic economic jihad against the West, and he is working clandestine operations to secure the fortunes of Islam at the expense of the West and the New World Order.

As David Jonsson wrote in 2006: "Islamic Economics is the stealth sword of Islam. It is more powerful than the Weapons of Mass Destruction and terrorism. It is immune to negotiation. The stealth sword is being applied for the Islamization of the West and the whole world. The goal is to create the *"Islamic kingdom of God on earth."* The implementation of *Shariah* law would have a dramatic affect on your life and that of the entire Western Civilization. Understand the nature of the evil and do not be blindsided."[32]

---

[32] David J. Jonsson, Islamic Economics and Shariah Law: A Plan for World Domination,

Jonsson goes on to write that "Islamic economics has an impact on your life, whether you are a banker, investing in the stock market, selling a home, buying a car, purchasing food, buying a suit or a dress, or just trying to make sense of the current events. Islamic economics and Islamic banking are primary Islamist strategies to condition the West to accept *Shariah* law as a basis for all life in all nations."[33]

It is important to recognize that the crippling of the American economy is part and parcel of the goal to establish a Shariah economic system not just over this nation, but worldwide. Jonsson said back in 2006

December 21, 2006.
http://www.salemthesoldier.us/jonsson_shariah_econ
omics.html

[33] Op. cit.

that "the Islamic movement is an idea movement" that "at the present time the leader(s) has not been identified."[34] I think the leader has now been identified, as he and his staff work tirelessly to achieve the ends of this economic jihad against American and the West.

As Jonsson put it: "The people in the West who are trying to construct a new socialism, a de-Marxified alternative to the politics of pure individualism, share the views of Islamist economists. These Westerners also accept the market as the essential driving-force of any economy, but they too wish to set it within a man-made moral framework that will ensure support for the weak through the compassion and self-

---

[34] Op. cit.

discipline of the strong. What communism tried and failed to achieve through the state, one Islamic economist has written, "is to be established through the agency of man himself." It would be a good slogan for the possible new socialism of the twenty-first century. As we will see, these principles are being promoted broadly in the West. This merging of ideologies is a powerful force in today's political environment. This merging is taking the form of a *Marxist/Leftist - Islamist Alliance*."[35]

I speak on this more in my book *Behold! A Red Horse!* This book is a must read for those who can't get enough of the four horsemen of the Apocalypse.

---

[35] Op. cit.

Empowering Turkey to Reestablish the Ottoman Empire

I have made the claim that Obama seeks to further the ambitions of the Turks to reestablish the Caliphate – the Ottoman Empire, and that he is working in a clandestine way to accomplish this goal as a closet jihadist working on behalf of Islam at the expense of the West. Let's see if the facts as they can be readily found play any of this out.

As of this writing, Obama will be meeting again with Turkey's Erdogan on December 7 (that's Pearl Harbor Day, in case you're wondering) to discuss . . . "strategies for Turkey's further involvement in

Afghanistan and Pakistan."[36] Turkey expects to reassert its influence over Tadzhikistan, Uzbekistan, Kyrgyzstan, Kazakhstan, Turkmenistan, Afghanistan and Pakistan by introducing a "secular" Islamic model over the top of the Taliban fundamental model.

The Islamic nations of Tadzhikistan, Uzbekistan, Kyrgyzstan, Kazakhstan, Turkmenistan, Afghanistan and Pakistan are all intended to fall under Turkish influence and control as the Ottoman alliances are recreated in furtherance of reestablishing the Islamic Kingdom under a single Caliph –the nations of Islam united under a new Caliphate. This influence may also reach well into Russia herself, including the Islamic

---

[36] http://www.hurriyetdailynews.com/n.php?n=obama-to-welcome-turkish-prime-minister-to-white-house-on-2009-10-30

Oblasts of Dagestan, Chechnya, Ingushetia, Kabardino-Balkaria and Cherkassy.

Erdoğan and Obama meet at the G-20 Pittsburgh summit in September.

This does not complete the authorization to rebuild, however. When Obama met with Erdoğan at the G20 summit, additional strategies were discussed.[37] There was discussion about the Upper Karabakh – a

---

37 http://www.trtenglish.com/trtinternational/en/newsDetail.aspx?HaberKodu=3e413a41-a9c2-440d-b74e-b329932c2e3b

disjointed piece of property to the south of Armenia, claimed by both Armenia and Azerbaijan, but occupied currently by Armenia. The willingness to discuss Turkey's influence on the Upper Karabakh while ignoring the issue of genocide against the Armenians in the last hours of the Ottoman Empire speaks volumes.

Erdoğan must have considered himself empowered, because when he left the G20, he proceeded to New York where he attended a reception given on the occasion of the 40th anniversary of the foundation of the Organization of the Islamic Conference, OIC, and held talks with UN Secretary General Ban Ki-moon.

Since that time, and with the full permission and authority of the United States' Executive Branch, Erdoğan has formed a high level cooperation council with Pakistan on October 25, 2009, consolidated Turkey's alliance with Muslim Azerbaijan, calling the Azeri flag and territories "holy" (Dar-es-salaam) on October 23, 2009, which is tantamount to a declaration of jihad against Armenia (a Christian nation).

Iraqi Prime Minister Nouri al-Maliki (R) greets his Turkish counterpart, Recep Tayyip Erdoğan, at Baghdad International Airport upon his arrival in Iraq.

But in case you think this is the worst of it, consider that on October 16, 2009,

Turkey signed accords with Iraq for regional integration.[38] Under these 48 accords, visa requirements and trans-border restrictions are all but abolished as though the two nations were . . . one empire.

Let's continue, shall we? On October 13, 2009, Turkey signed a 38 point accord with Syria that ended visa restrictions and travel between the two countries. The arrangement is more or less borderless. The vehicle used for this accord was something called the Turkey-Syria High Level Strategic Cooperation Council.[39]

Securing Jerusalem from the Israelis

---

[38]

http://merryabla64.wordpress.com/2009/10/16/turkey-iraq-sign-accords-for-regional-integration/

[39]

http://www.interesclub.org/home/3417.html?task=view

However, no sooner did Erdoğan wrap up the initial phase of the alliance between Turkey and Azerbaijan, Syria, Iraq, Iran, Tadzhikistan, Uzbekistan, Kyrgyzstan, Kazakhstan, Turkmenistan, Afghanistan and Pakistan (the nations ending with "Stan" are referred to in the bible as the lands of "Magog"), then Ban Ki-moon starts to press for international control over Jerusalem.[40]

Ban Ki-moon is pushing to make Jerusalem the capitol of both the Palestinian state and Israel, in order to make the holy sites acceptable to all. He stressed that the international community does not recognize Israel's annexation of East Jerusalem.

---

[40] http://www.scoop.co.nz/stories/WO0910/S00421.htm

To make matters worse, Obama now wants a cram down, forcing the Israelis to accept the creation of Jerusalem as the capitol of the new Palestinian state as a unilateral move without Israeli approval. See "Obama green-lights Arab land grab", Aaron Klein, WorldNetDaily, November 15, 2009.

The One is moving well along his agenda, which is *inconsistent* with the agenda of his mentors, a total violation of his duty to the United States of America, a betrayal of his oath of office, and a betrayal of the Western world. He is on the precipice of completely destroying the American economy for generations. He has already launched Turkey into a full court press to reestablish the Islamic Caliphate whose capitol will be Jerusalem, and he is well underway to securing Jerusalem from the Israelis,

notwithstanding their objections

> How art thou fallen from heaven, O
> Lucifer, son of the morning! How art
> thou cut down to the ground, which
> didst weaken the nations! For thou
> hast said in thine heart, I will ascend
> into heaven, I will exalt **my throne**
> above the stars of God: I will sit also
> upon **the mount of the congregation**,
> in the sides of **the north**:
>
>   - Isaiah 14:12-13

CHAPTER TWENTY

The lawless acts of Barack Hussein Obama

It is now necessary to consider the unlawful – the lawless – acts of Barack Hussein Obama, ignoring entirely the issue of his birth.

Violations of the Logan Act.

We begin with the Logan Act, 18 USC 953 - Sec. 953. Private correspondence with foreign governments:

> *Any citizen of the United States, wherever he may be, who, without authority of the United States, directly or indirectly commences or carries on any correspondence or intercourse with any foreign government or any officer or agent thereof, with intent to influence the measures or conduct of*

any foreign government or of any officer or agent thereof, in relation to any disputes or controversies with the United States, or to defeat the measures of the United States, shall be fined under this title or imprisoned not more than three years, or both. This section shall not abridge the right of a citizen to apply, himself or his agent, to any foreign government or the agents thereof for redress of any injury which he may have sustained from such government or any of its agents or subjects.

GeostrategyDirect.com, a newsletter published by Bill Gertz stated in a piece of February 3, 2009,[41] that "Diplomatic sources

---

[41] GAFFNEY: S-U-B-M-I-S-S-I-O-N, Frank Gaffney, Washington Times, February 3, 2009

said Barack Obama has engaged several Arab intermediaries to relay **messages to and from al Qaeda** in the months before his elections as the 44th U.S. president. The sources said al Qaeda **has offered what they termed a truce in exchange for a U.S. military withdrawal from Afghanistan**.

"For the last few months, Obama has been receiving and sending feelers to those close to al Qaeda on whether the group would end its terrorist campaign against the United States,' a diplomatic source said. 'Obama sees this as helpful to his plans to essentially withdraw from Afghanistan and Iraq during his first term in office.'

"If surrender in Afghanistan, Iraq and Iran were not enough, upcoming opportunities for Mr. Obama to exhibit American submission to Islam include ordering U.S. participation in the United Nations' 'Durban II' conference - thereby legitimating its Iranian-dictated, rabidly anti-Israel, anti-American, Holocaust-denying and 'Islamophobia' -banning agenda; adopting the program for undermining Israel promoted by longtime Friends-of-Barack Rashid Khalidi and Samantha Power (the latter just appointed a senior National Security Council official); and reversing the FBI's long-overdue decision to end its association with the Council on American Islamic Relations (CAIR), a prominent front organization of the Muslim Brotherhood (whose stated mission is 'to destroy America from within.')"

These are the facts as published, and which remain undisputed to this day. Now, let's take a look again at the elements of the Logan Act in relation to these facts as alleged:

Elements:

- Obama claims to be a Citizen of the United States
- He was never authorized to engage in discussions with al Qaeda prior to his election to the office of the Presidency
- He directly commenced and carried on correspondence or intercourse with members of al Qaeda
- He did so with the intent to influence the measures or conduct of any foreign government or of any officer or agent thereof, in relation to any disputes or controversies with the United States, or to defeat the measures of the United States.

You can conclude for yourself whether a violation of the Logan Act occurred.

Fraud and False Statements.

18 U.S.C. § 1002 - Fraud and False Statements - Possession of false papers to defraud United States, provides severe criminal penalties for fraud and false statements using false papers in order to defraud the United States, to wit:

(c) Whoever uses or attempts to use **any certificate** of arrival, declaration of intention, certificate of naturalization, certificate of citizenship **or other documentary evidence** . . . **of citizenship**, **or any duplicate or copy thereof**, knowing the same to have been procured by fraud or false evidence . . .; or

(d) Whoever knowingly **makes any false certificate** . . .; or

(e) Whoever knowingly makes any false statement or claim that he is, or at any time has been, a citizen or national of the United States, with the intent to obtain on behalf of himself, . . ., any Federal or State benefit or service, or to engage unlawfully in employment in the United States;

Shall be fined under this title **or imprisoned** not more than **five years**, or both.

Also consider 18 U.S.C. § 1017 – Fraud and False Statements - Government seals wrongfully used and instruments wrongfully sealed. This federal statute also provides for five years in prison for "whoever fraudulently or wrongfully affixes or impresses the seal of any department or agency of the United States, to or upon any certificate," or "whoever knowingly and without lawful authority produces an identification document, authentication feature, or a false identification document.

However, the federal government takes identity fraud very seriously. Under 18 U.S.C. § 1028 - Fraud and related activity in connection with identification documents, authentication features, and information, the punishment for an offense under subsection (a) of this section is a fine or imprisonment for not more than 15 years, or both, **if the offense is** the production or transfer of an identification document, authentication feature, or false identification document that is or appears to be . . . **a birth certificate,** or a driver's license or personal identification card.

Obama prior to his election, initially caused to be produced the following Certification of Live Birth:

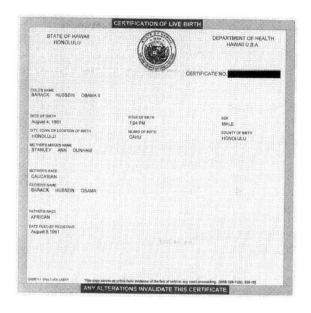

CERTIFICATION OF LIVE BIRTH

STATE OF HAWAII
HONOLULU

DEPARTMENT OF HEALTH
HAWAII U.S.A.

CERTIFICATE NO.

CHILD'S NAME
BARACK HUSSEIN OBAMA II

DATE OF BIRTH
August 4, 1961

HOUR OF BIRTH
7:24 PM

SEX
MALE

CITY, TOWN OR LOCATION OF BIRTH
HONOLULU

ISLAND OF BIRTH
OAHU

COUNTY OF BIRTH
HONOLULU

MOTHER'S MAIDEN NAME
STANLEY ANN DUNHAM

MOTHER'S RACE
CAUCASIAN

FATHER'S NAME
BARACK HUSSEIN OBAMA

FATHER'S RACE
AFRICAN

DATE FILED BY REGISTRAR
August 8, 1961

This copy serves as prima facie evidence of the fact of birth in any court proceeding. [HRS 338-13(b), 338-19]

ANY ALTERATIONS INVALIDATE THIS CERTIFICATE

This document has been determined to be a forgery by at least two internationally respected computer forensic auditors. Whether or not it is a forgery, there are some obvious things about this COLB. First, it provides on the bottom that "Any Alterations Invalidate This Certificate." A quick review indicates that the Certificate No. has been blacked out. It is therefore altered, and therefore invalid. Nonetheless, this is the document that Chris Matthews heralded as proof that Obama was born in Hawaii, and this is the document that Bill O'Reilly claimed was in his possession (he incorrectly called it a birth certificate).

There are other glaring deficiencies with this document as well, including the failure to evidence a raised embossed seal from the State of Hawaii (a clear indication of a faked document), and the signature of an Hawaiian authority signing the seal. The document is not creased as a mailed document would be, and the "hard copy" was never produced – just an internet posting.

As we all know, if you get two different stories from a suspect, at least one of the stories is a lie. After the DNC and most of the news broadcasters had concluded that Obama was born in Hawaii based on this forgery, FactCheck.org released another internet image of a completely different document, claiming that this time, the Certification of Live Birth was genuine.

Before reviewing this document, it is important to know that Barack Obama and William Ayers served together on the Philanthropic Woods Foundation Board, a foundation that controls FactCheck.org. Here is what FactCheck.org produced:

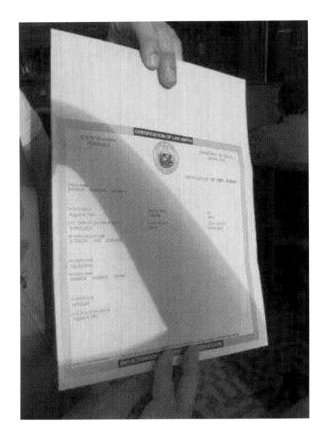

Magically, the black line over the Certificate Number is gone. This document is creased and it contains a state seal, although

the seal and the whole document cannot be
seen in the same photograph:

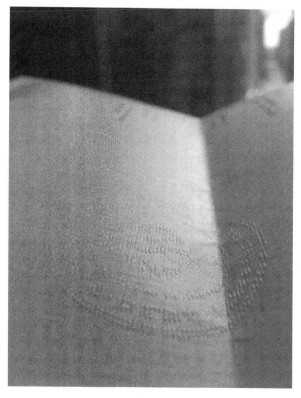

Two separate COLBs, and two
separate images means at least one of them

was a fraud, and between the two, document number one is a clear qualifier, although document number 2 has also been proven a fake. Take a look at 18 U.S.C. § 1028 one more time. The penalty for violating this statute with the intent to secure anything from the United States can be punishable with up to fifteen years in prison.

United Nations General Assembly Resolution 181

November 29, 1947

The General Assembly, Having met in special session at the request of the mandatory Power to constitute and instruct a Special Committee to prepare for the consideration of the question of the future Government of Palestine at the second regular session;

Having constituted a Special Committee and instructed it to investigate all questions and issues relevant to the problem of Palestine, and to prepare proposals for the solution of the problem, and

Having received and examined the report of the Special Committee (document A/364)[1] including a number of unanimous recommendations and a plan of partition with economic union approved by the majority of the Special Committee,

Considers that the present situation in Palestine is one which is likely to impair the general welfare and friendly relations among nations;

Takes note of the declaration by the mandatory Power that it plans to complete its evacuation of Palestine by 1 August 1948;

Recommends to the United Kingdom, as the mandatory Power for Palestine, and to all other Members of the United Nations the adoption and implementation, with regard to the future Government of Palestine, of the Plan of Partition with Economic Union set out below;

Requests that

The Security Council take the necessary measures as provided for in the plan for its implementation;

The Security Council consider, if circumstances during the transitional period require such consideration, whether the situation in Palestine constitutes a threat to the peace. If it decides that such a threat exists, and in order to maintain international peace and security, the Security Council should supplement the authorization of the General Assembly by taking measures, under Articles 39 and 41 of the Charter, to empower the United Nations Commission, as provided in this resolution, to exercise in Palestine the functions which are assigned to it by this resolution;

The Security Council determine as a threat to the peace, breach of the peace or act of aggression, in accordance with <u>Article 39 of the Charter</u>, any attempt to alter by force the settlement envisaged by this resolution;

The Trusteeship Council be informed of the responsibilities envisaged for it in this plan;

Calls upon the inhabitants of Palestine to take such steps as may be necessary on their part to put this plan into effect;

Appeals to all Governments and all peoples to refrain from taking any action which might hamper or delay the carrying out of these recommendations, and

Authorizes the Secretary-General to reimburse travel and subsistence expenses of the members of the Commission referred to in Part 1, Section B, Paragraph I below, on such basis and in such form as he may determine most appropriate in the circumstances, and to provide the Commission with the necessary staff to assist in carrying out the functions assigned to the Commission by the General Assembly.*

The General Assembly,

Authorizes the Secretary-General to draw from the Working Capital Fund a sum not to exceed 2,000,000 dollars for the purposes set forth in the last paragraph of the resolution on the future government of Palestine.

PLAN OF PARTITION WITH ECONOMIC UNION

Part I. - Future Constitution and Government of Palestine

A. TERMINATION OF MANDATE, PARTITION AND INDEPENDENCE

The <u>Mandate for Palestine</u> shall terminate as soon as possible but in any case not later than 1 August 1948.

The armed forces of the mandatory Power shall be progressively withdrawn from Palestine, the withdrawal to be completed as soon as possible but in any case not later than 1 August 1948.

The mandatory Power shall advise the Commission, as far in advance as possible, of its intention to terminate the mandate and to evacuate each area. The mandatory Power shall use its best endeavours to ensure that an area situated in the territory of the Jewish State, including a seaport and hinterland adequate to provide facilities for a substantial immigration, shall be evacuated at the earliest possible date and in any event not later than 1 February 1948.

Independent Arab and Jewish States and the Special International Regime for the City of Jerusalem, set forth in Part III of this Plan, shall come into existence in Palestine two months after the evacuation of the armed forces of the mandatory Power has been completed but in any case not later than 1 October 1948. The boundaries of the Arab State, the Jewish State, and the City of Jerusalem shall be as described in Parts II and III below.

The period between the adoption by the General Assembly of its recommendation on the question of Palestine and the establishment of the independence of the Arab and Jewish States shall be a transitional period.

B. STEPS PREPARATORY TO INDEPENDENCE

A Commission shall be set up consisting of one representative of each of five Member States. The Members represented on the Commission shall be elected by the General Assembly on as broad a basis, geographically and otherwise, as possible.

The administration of Palestine shall, as the mandatory Power withdraws its armed forces, be progressively turned over to the Commission, which shall act in conformity with the recommendations of the General

Assembly, under the guidance of the Security Council. The mandatory Power shall to the fullest possible extent coordinate its plans for withdrawal with the plans of the Commission to take over and administer areas which have been evacuated.

In the discharge of this administrative responsibility the Commission shall have authority to issue necessary regulations and take other measures as required.

The mandatory Power shall not take any action to prevent, obstruct or delay the implementation by the Commission of the measures recommended by the General Assembly.

On its arrival in Palestine the Commission shall proceed to carry out measures for the establishment of the frontiers of the Arab and Jewish States and the City of Jerusalem in accordance with the general lines of the recommendations of the General Assembly on the partition of Palestine. Nevertheless, the boundaries as described in Part II of this Plan are to be modified in such a way that village areas as a rule will not be divided by state boundaries unless pressing reasons make that necessary.

The Commission, after consultation with the democratic parties and other public organizations of the Arab and Jewish States, shall select and establish in each State as rapidly as possible a Provisional Council of Government. The activities of both the Arab and Jewish Provisional Councils of Government shall be carried out under the general direction of the Commission.

If by 1 April 1948 a Provisional Council of Government cannot be selected for either of the States, or, if selected, cannot carry out its functions, the Commission shall communicate that fact to the Security Council for such action with respect to that State as the Security Council may deem proper, and to the Secretary-General for communication to the Members of the United Nations.

Subject to the provisions of these recommendations, during the transitional period the Provisional Councils of Government, acting under the Commission, shall have full authority in the areas under their control including authority over matters of immigration and land regulation.

The Provisional Council of Government of each State, acting under the Commission, shall progressively receive from the Commission full responsibility for the administration of that State in the period between the termination of the Mandate and the establishment of the State's independence.

The Commission shall instruct the Provisional Councils of Government of both the Arab and Jewish States, after their formation, to proceed to the establishment of administrative organs of government, central and local.

The Provisional Council of Government of each State shall, within the shortest time possible, recruit an armed militia from the residents of that State, sufficient in number to maintain internal order and to prevent frontier clashes.

This armed militia in each State shall, for operational purposes, be under the command of Jewish or Arab officers resident in that State, but general political and military control, including the choice of the militia's High Command, shall be exercised by the Commission.

The Provisional Council of Government of each State shall, not later than two months after the withdrawal of the armed forces of the mandatory Power, hold elections to the Constituent Assembly which shall be conducted on democratic lines.

The election regulations in each State shall be drawn up by the Provisional Council of Government and approved by the Commission. Qualified voters for each State for this election shall be persons over eighteen years of age who are (a) Palestinian citizens residing in that State; and (b) Arabs and Jews residing in the State, although not Palestinian citizens, who, before voting, have signed a notice of intention to become citizens of such State.

Arabs and Jews residing in the City of Jerusalem who have signed a notice of intention to become citizens, the Arabs of the

Arab State and the Jews of the Jewish State, shall be entitled to vote in the Arab and Jewish States respectively.

Women may vote and be elected to the Constituent Assemblies.

During the transitional period no Jew shall be permitted to establish residence in the area of the proposed Arab State, and no Arab shall be permitted to establish residence in the area of the proposed Jewish State, except by special leave of the Commission.

The Constituent Assembly of each State shall draft a democratic constitution for its State and choose a provisional government to succeed the Provisional Council of Government appointed by the Commission. The Constitutions of the States shall embody Chapters 1 and 2 of the Declaration provided for in section C below and include, inter alia, provisions for:

Establishing in each State a legislative body elected by universal suffrage and by secret ballot on the basis of proportional representation, and an executive body responsible to the legislature;

Settling all international disputes in which the State may be involved by peaceful means in such a manner that international peace and security, and justice, are not endangered;

Accepting the obligation of the State to refrain in its international relations from the threat or use of force against the territorial integrity or political independence of any State, or in any other manner inconsistent with the purpose of the United Nations;

Guaranteeing to all persons equal and non-discriminatory rights in civil, political, economic and religious matters and the enjoyment of human rights and fundamental freedoms, including freedom of religion, language, speech and publication, education, assembly and association;

Preserving freedom of transit and visit for all residents and citizens of the other State in Palestine and the City of Jerusalem, subject to considerations of national security, provided that each State shall control residence within its borders.

The Commission shall appoint a preparatory economic commission of three members to make whatever arrangements are possible for economic co-operation, with a view to establishing, as soon as practicable, the Economic Union and the Joint Economic Board, as provided in section D below.

During the period between the adoption of the recommendations on the question of Palestine by the General Assembly and the termination of the Mandate, the mandatory Power in Palestine shall maintain full responsibility for administration in areas from which it has not withdrawn its armed forces. The Commission shall assist the mandatory Power in the carrying out of these functions. Similarly the mandatory Power shall co-operate with the Commission in the execution of its functions.

With a view to ensuring that there shall be continuity in the functioning of administrative services and that, on the withdrawal of the armed forces of the mandatory Power, the whole administration shall be in the charge of the Provisional Councils and the Joint Economic Board, respectively, acting under the Commission, there shall be a progressive transfer, from the mandatory Power to the Commission, of responsibility for all the functions of government, including that of maintaining law and order in the areas from which the forces of the mandatory Power have been withdrawn.

The Commission shall be guided in its activities by the recommendations of the General Assembly and by such instructions as the Security Council may consider necessary to issue.

The measures taken by the Commission, within the recommendations of the General Assembly, shall become immediately effective unless the Commission has previously received contrary instructions from the Security Council.

The Commission shall render periodic monthly progress reports, or more frequently if desirable, to the Security Council.

The Commission shall make its final report to the next regular session of the General Assembly and to the Security Council simultaneously.

C. DECLARATION

A declaration shall be made to the United Nations by the Provisional Government of each proposed State before independence. It shall contain, inter alia, the following clauses:

General Provision

The stipulations contained in the Declaration are recognized as fundamental laws of the State and no law, regulation or official action shall conflict or interfere with these stipulations, nor shall any law, regulation or official action prevail over them.

Chapter 1: Holy Places, Religious Buildings and Sites

Existing rights in respect of Holy Places and religious buildings or sites shall not be denied or impaired.

In so far as Holy Places are concerned, the liberty of access, visit, and transit shall be guaranteed, in conformity with existing rights, to all residents and citizen of the other State and of the City of Jerusalem, as well as to aliens, without distinction as to nationality, subject to requirements of national security, public order and decorum.

Similarly, freedom of worship shall be guaranteed in conformity with existing rights, subject to the maintenance of public order and decorum.

Holy Places and religious buildings or sites shall be preserved. No act shall be permitted which may in an way impair their sacred character. If at any time it appears to the Government that any particular Holy Place, religious, building or site is in need of urgent repair, the Government may call upon the community or communities concerned to carry out such repair. The Government may carry it out itself at the expense of the community or community concerned if no action is taken within a reasonable time.

No taxation shall be levied in respect of any Holy Place, religious building or site which was exempt from taxation on the date of the creation of the State.

No change in the incidence of such taxation shall be made which would either discriminate between the owners or occupiers of Holy Places, religious buildings or sites, or would place such owners or occupiers in a position less favourable in relation to the general incidence of taxation than existed at the time of the adoption of the Assembly's recommendations.

The Governor of the City of Jerusalem shall have the right to determine whether the provisions of the Constitution of the State in relation to Holy Places, religious buildings and sites within the borders of the State and the religious rights appertaining thereto, are being properly applied and respected, and to make decisions on the basis of existing rights in cases of disputes which may arise between the different religious communities or the rites of a religious community with respect to such places, buildings and sites. He shall receive full co-operation and such privileges and immunities as are necessary for the exercise of his functions in the State.

Chapter 2: Religious and Minority Rights

Freedom of conscience and the free exercise of all forms of worship, subject only to the maintenance of public order and morals, shall be ensured to all.

No discrimination of any kind shall be made between the inhabitants on the ground of race, religion, language or sex.

All persons within the jurisdiction of the State shall be entitled to equal protection of the laws.

The family law and personal status of the various minorities and their religious interests, including endowments, shall be respected.

Except as may be required for the maintenance of public order and good government, no measure shall be taken to obstruct or interfere with the enterprise of religious or charitable bodies of all faiths or to discriminate against any representative or member of these bodies on the ground of his religion or nationality.

The State shall ensure adequate primary and secondary education for the Arab and Jewish minority, respectively, in its own language and its cultural traditions.

The right of each community to maintain its own schools for the education of its own members in its own language, while conforming to such educational requirements of a general nature as the State may impose, shall not be denied or impaired. Foreign educational establishments shall continue their activity on the basis of their existing rights.

No restriction shall be imposed on the free use by any citizen of the State of any language in private intercourse, in commerce, in religion, in the Press or in publications of any kind, or at public meetings.[3]

No expropriation of land owned by an Arab in the Jewish State (by a Jew in the Arab State)[4] shall be allowed except for public purposes. In all cases of expropriation full compensation as fixed by the Supreme Court shall be said previous to dispossession.

Chapter 3: Citizenship, International Conventions and Financial Obligations

1. Citizenship Palestinian citizens residing in Palestine outside the City of Jerusalem, as well as Arabs and Jews who, not holding Palestinian citizenship, reside in Palestine outside the City of Jerusalem shall, upon the recognition of independence, become citizens of the State in which they are resident and enjoy full civil and political rights. Persons over the age of eighteen years may opt, within one year from the date of recognition of independence of the State in which they reside, for citizenship of the other State, providing that no Arab residing in the area of the proposed Arab State shall have the right to opt for citizenship in the proposed Jewish State and no Jew residing in the proposed Jewish State shall have the right to opt for citizenship in the proposed Arab State. The exercise of this right of option will be taken to include the wives and children under eighteen years of age of persons so opting.

Arabs residing in the area of the proposed Jewish State and Jews residing in the area of the proposed Arab State who have signed a notice of intention to opt for citizenship of the other State shall be eligible to vote in the elections to the Constituent Assembly of that State, but not in the elections to the Constituent Assembly of the State in which they reside.

2. International conventions

The State shall be bound by all the international agreements and conventions, both general and special, to which Palestine has become a party. Subject to any right of denunciation provided for therein, such agreements and conventions shall be respected by the State throughout the period for which they were concluded.

Any dispute about the applicability and continued validity of international conventions or treaties signed or adhered to by the mandatory Power on behalf of Palestine shall be referred to the International Court of Justice in accordance with the provisions of the Statute of the Court.

3. Financial obligations

The State shall respect and fulfil all financial obligations of whatever nature assumed on behalf of Palestine by the mandatory Power during the exercise of the Mandate and recognized by the State. This provision includes the right of public servants to pensions, compensation or gratuities.

These obligations shall be fulfilled through participation in the Joint Economic Board in respect of those obligations applicable to Palestine as a whole, and individually in respect of those applicable to, and fairly apportionable between, the States.

A Court of Claims, affiliated with the Joint Economic Board, and composed of one member appointed by the United Nations, one representative of the United Kingdom and one representative of the State concerned, should be established. Any dispute between the United Kingdom and the

State respecting claims not recognized by the latter should be referred to that Court.

Commercial concessions granted in respect of any part of Palestine prior to the adoption of the resolution by the General Assembly shall continue to be valid according to their terms, unless modified by agreement between the concession-holders and the State.

Chapter 4: Miscellaneous Provisions

The provisions of chapters 1 and 2 of the declaration shall be under the guarantee of the United Nations, and no modifications shall be made in them without the assent of the General Assembly of the United Nations. Any Member of the United Nations shall have the right to bring to the attention of the General Assembly any infraction or danger of infraction of any of these stipulations, and the General Assembly may thereupon make such recommendations as it may deem proper in the circumstances.

Any dispute relating to the application or interpretation of this declaration shall be

referred, at the request of either party, to the
International Court of Justice, unless the
parties agree to another mode of settlement.

D. ECONOMIC UNION AND TRANSIT

The Provisional Council of Government of
each State shall enter into an undertaking
with respect to Economic Union and Transit.
This undertaking shall be drafted by the
Commission provided for in section B,
paragraph 1, utilizing to the greatest possible
extent the advice and cooperation of
representative organizations and bodies from
each of the proposed States. It shall contain
provisions to establish the Economic Union of
Palestine and provide for other matters of
common interest. If by 1 April 1948 the
Provisional Councils of Government have not
entered into the undertaking, the
undertaking shall be put into force by the
Commission.

The Economic Union of Palestine

The objectives of the Economic Union of
Palestine shall be:

A customs union;

A joint currency system providing for a single foreign exchange rate;

Operation in the common interest on a non-discriminatory basis of railways inter-State highways; postal, telephone and telegraphic services and ports and airports involved in international trade and commerce;

Joint economic development, especially in respect of irrigation, land reclamation and soil conservation;

Access for both States and for the City of Jerusalem on a non-discriminatory basis to water and power facilities.

There shall be established a Joint Economic Board, which shall consist of three representatives of each of the two States and three foreign members appointed by the Economic and Social Council of the United Nations. The foreign members shall be appointed in the first instance for a term of three years; they shall serve as individuals and not as representatives of States.

The functions of the Joint Economic Board shall be to implement either directly or by delegation the measures necessary to realize the objectives of the Economic Union. It shall have all powers of organization and administration necessary to fulfil its functions.

The States shall bind themselves to put into effect the decisions of the Joint Economic Board. The Board's decisions shall be taken by a majority vote.

In the event of failure of a State to take the necessary action the Board may, by a vote of six members, decide to withhold an appropriate portion of the part of the customs revenue to which the State in question is entitled under the Economic Union. Should the State persist in its failure to cooperate, the Board may decide by a simple majority vote upon such further sanctions, including disposition of funds which it has withheld, as it may deem appropriate.

In relation to economic development, the functions of the Board shall be planning, investigation and encouragement of joint development projects, but it shall not undertake such projects except with the assent of both States and the City of Jerusalem, in the event that Jerusalem is directly involved in the development project.

In regard to the joint currency system, the currencies circulating in the two States and the City of Jerusalem shall be issued under the authority of the Joint Economic Board, which shall be the sole issuing authority and which shall determine the reserves to be held against such currencies.

So far as is consistent with paragraph 2(b) above, each State may operate its own central bank, control its own fiscal and credit policy, its foreign exchange receipts and expenditures, the grant of import licences, and may conduct international financial operations on its own faith and credit. During the first two years after the termination of the Mandate, the Joint Economic Board shall have the authority to take such measures as may be necessary to ensure that - to the extent that the total foreign exchange revenues of the two States from the export of goods and services permit, and provided that each State takes appropriate measures to conserve its own foreign exchange resources - each State shall have available, in any twelve months' period, foreign exchange sufficient to assure the supply of quantities of imported goods and services for consumption in its territory equivalent to the quantities of such goods and services consumed in that territory in the twelve months' period ending 31 December 1947.

All economic authority not specifically vested in the Joint Economic Board is reserved to each State.

There shall be a common customs tariff with complete freedom of trade between the States, and between the States and the City of Jerusalem.

The tariff schedules shall be drawn up by a Tariff Commission, consisting of representatives of each of the States in equal numbers, and shall be submitted to the Joint Economic Board for approval by a majority vote. In case of disagreement in the Tariff Commission, the Joint Economic Board shall arbitrate the points of difference. In the event that the Tariff Commission fails to draw up any schedule by a date to bc fixed, the Joint Economic Board shall determine the tariff schedule.

The following items shall be a first charge on the customs and other common revenue of the Joint Economic Board:

The expenses of the customs service and of the operation of the joint services;

The administrative expenses of the Joint Economic Board;

The financial obligations of the Administration of Palestine, consisting of:

The service of the outstanding public debt;

The cost of superannuation benefits, now being paid or falling due in the future, in accordance with the rules and to the extent established by paragraph 3 of chapter 3 above.

After these obligations have been met in full, the surplus revenue from the customs and other common services shall be divided in the following manner: not less than 5 per cent and not more than 10 per cent to the City of Jerusalem; the residue shall be allocated to each State by the Joint Economic Board equitably, with the objective of maintaining a sufficient and suitable level of government and social services in each State, except that the share of either State shall not exceed the amount of that State's contribution to the revenues of the Economic Union by more than approximately four million pounds in any year. The amount granted may be adjusted by the Board according to the price level in relation to the prices prevailing at the time of the establishment of the Union. After five years, the principles of the distribution of the joint revenue may be revised by the Joint Economic Board on a basis of equity.

All international conventions and treaties affecting customs tariff rates, and those communications services under the jurisdiction of the Joint Economic Board, shall be entered into by both States. In these matters, the two States shall be bound to act in accordance with the majority of the Joint Economic Board.

The Joint Economic Board shall endeavour to secure for Palestine's exports fair and equal access to world markets.

All enterprises operated by the Joint Economic Board shall pay fair wages on a uniform basis.

Freedom of Transit and Visit

▢ The undertaking shall contain provisions preserving freedom of transit and visit for all residents or citizens of both States and of the City of Jerusalem, subject to security considerations; provided that each State and the City shall control residence within its borders.

Termination, Modification and Interpretation of the Undertaking

The undertaking and any treaty issuing therefrom shall remain in force for a period of ten years. It shall continue in force until notice of termination, to take effect two years thereafter, is given by either of the parties.

During the initial ten-year period, the undertaking and any treaty issuing therefrom may not be modified except by consent of both parties and with the approval of the General Assembly.

Any dispute relating to the application or the interpretation of the undertaking and any treaty issuing therefrom shall be referred, at the request of either party, to the International Court Of Justice, unless the parties agree to another mode of settlement.

E. ASSETS

The movable assets of the Administration of Palestine shall be allocated to the Arab and Jewish States and the City of Jerusalem on an equitable basis. Allocations should be made by the United Nations Commission referred to iii section B, paragraph 1, above. Immovable assets shall become the property of the government of the territory in which they are situated.

During the period between the appointment of the United Nations Commission and the termination of the Mandate, the mandatory Power shall, except in respect of ordinary operations, consult with the Commission on any measure which it may contemplate involving the liquidation, disposal or encumbering of the assets of the Palestine Government, such as the accumulated treasury surplus, the proceeds of Government bond issues, State lands or any other asset.

F. ADMISSION TO MEMBERSHIP IN THE UNITED NATIONS

When the independence of either the Arab or the Jewish State as envisaged in this plan has become effective and the declaration and undertaking, as envisaged in this plan, have been signed by either of them, sympathetic consideration should be given to its application for admission to membership in the United Nations in accordance with article 4 of the Charter of the United Nations.

Part II. - Boundaries

A. THE ARAB STATE

The area of the Arab State in Western Galilee is bounded on the west by the Mediterranean and on the north by the frontier of the Lebanon from Ras en Naqura to a point north of Saliha. From there the boundary proceeds southwards, leaving the built-up area of Saliha in the Arab State, to join the southernmost point of this village. There it follows the western boundary line of the villages of 'Alma, Rihaniya and Teitaba, thence following the northern boundary line of Meirun village to join the Acre-Safad Sub-District boundary line. It follows this line to a point west of Es Sammu'i village and joins it again at the northernmost point of Farradiya. Thence it follows the sub-district boundary line to the Acre-Safad main road. From here it follows the western boundary of Kafr-I'nan village until it reaches the Tiberias-Acre Sub-District boundary line, passing to the west of the junction of the Acre-Safad and Lubiya-Kafr-I'nan roads. From the south-west corner of Kafr-I'nan village the boundary line follows the western boundary of the Tiberias

Sub-District to a point close to the boundary line between the villages of Maghar and 'Eilabun, thence bulging out to the west to include as much of the eastern part of the plain of Battuf as is necessary for the reservoir proposed by the Jewish Agency for the irrigation of lands to the south and east.

The boundary rejoins the Tiberias Sub-District boundary at a point on the Nazareth-Tiberias road south-east of the built-up area of Tur'an; thence it runs southwards, at first following the sub-district boundary and then passing between the Kadoorie Agricultural School and Mount Tabor, to a point due south at the base of Mount Tabor. From here it runs due west, parallel to the horizontal grid line 230, to the north-east corner of the village lands of Tel Adashim. It then runs to the northwest corner of these lands, whence it turns south and west so as to include in the Arab State the sources of the Nazareth water supply in Yafa village. On reaching Ginneiger it follows the eastern, northern and western boundaries of the lands of this village to their south-west comer, whence it proceeds in a straight line to a point on the Haifa-Afula railway on the boundary between the villages of Sarid and El-Mujeidil. This is the point of intersection. The south-western boundary of the area of the Arab State in Galilee takes a line from this point, passing northwards along the eastern boundaries of Sarid and Gevat to the north-eastern corner of Nahalal, proceeding thence across the land of Kefar ha Horesh to a central point on the southern boundary of the village of 'Ilut, thence westwards along that village boundary to the eastern boundary of Beit Lahm, thence northwards and north-eastwards along its western boundary to the north-eastern corner of Waldheim and thence north-westwards across the village lands of Shafa 'Amr to the southeastern corner of Ramat Yohanan. From here it runs due north-north-east to a point on the Shafa 'Amr-Haifa road, west of its junction with the road of I'billin. From there it proceeds north-east to a point on the southern boundary of I'billin situated to the west of the I'billin-Birwa road. Thence along that boundary to its westernmost point, whence it turns to the north, follows across the village land of Tamra to the north-westernmost corner and along the western boundary of Julis until it reaches the Acre-Safad road. It then runs westwards along the southern side of the Safad-Acre road to the Galilee-Haifa District boundary, from which point it follows that boundary to the sea.

The boundary of the hill country of Samaria and Judea starts on the Jordan River at the Wadi Malih south-east of Beisan and runs due west to meet the Beisan-Jericho road and then follows the western side of that road in a north-westerly direction to the junction of the boundaries of the Sub-Districts of Beisan, Nablus, and Jenin. From that point it follows the Nablus-Jenin sub-District boundary westwards for a distance of about three kilometres and then turns north-westwards, passing to the east of the built-up areas of the villages of Jalbun and Faqqu'a, to the boundary of the Sub-Districts of Jenin and Beisan at a point northeast of Nuris. Thence it proceeds first northwestwards to a point due north of the built-up area of Zie'in and then westwards to the Afula-Jenin railway, thence north-westwards along the District boundary line to the point of intersection on the Hejaz railway. From here the boundary runs southwestwards, including the built-up area and some of the land of the village of Kh. Lid in the Arab State to cross the Haifa-Jenin road at a point on the district boundary between Haifa and Samaria west of El- Mansi. It follows this boundary to the southernmost point of the village of El-Buteimat. From here it follows the northern and eastern boundaries of the village of Ar'ara rejoining the Haifa-Samaria district boundary at Wadi 'Ara, and thence proceeding south-south-westwards in an approximately straight line joining up with the western boundary of Qaqun to a point east of the railway line on the eastern boundary of Qaqun village. From here it runs along the railway line some distance to the east of it to a point just east of the Tulkarm railway station. Thence the boundary follows a line half-way between the railway and the Tulkarm-Qalqiliya-Jaljuliya and Ras El-Ein road to a point just east of Ras El-Ein station, whence it proceeds along the railway some distance to the east of it to the point on the railway line south of the junction of the Haifa-Lydda and Beit Nabala lines, whence it proceeds along the southern border of Lydda airport to its south-west corner, thence in a south-westerly direction to a point just west of the built-up area of Sarafand El 'Amar, whence it turns south, passing just to the west of the built-up area of

Abu El-Fadil to the north-east corner of the lands of Beer Ya'aqov. (The boundary line should be so demarcated as to allow direct access from the Arab State to the airport.) Thence the boundary line follows the western and southern boundaries of Ramle village, to the north-east corner of El Na'ana village, thence in a straight line to the southernmost point of El Barriya, along the eastern boundary of that village and the southern boundary of 'Innaba village. Thence it turns north to follow the southern side of the Jaffa-Jerusalem road until El-Qubab, whence it follows the road to the boundary of Abu-Shusha. It runs along the eastern boundaries of Abu Shusha, Seidun, Hulda to the southernmost point of Hulda, thence westwards in a straight line to the north-eastern corner of Umm Kalkha, thence following the northern boundaries of Umm Kalkha, Qazaza and the northern and western boundaries of Mukhezin to the Gaza District boundary and thence runs across the village lands of El-Mismiya El-Kabira, and Yasur to the southern point of intersection, which is midway between the built-up areas of Yasur and Batani Sharqi.

From the southern point of intersection the boundary lines run north-westwards between the villages of Gan Yavne and Barqa to the sea at a point half way between Nabi Yunis and Minat El-Qila, and south-eastwards to a point west of Qastina, whence it turns in a south-westerly direction, passing to the east of the built-up areas of Es Sawafir Esh Sharqiya and 'Ibdis. From the south-east corner of 'Ibdis village it runs to a point southwest of the built-up area of Beit 'Affa, crossing the Hebron-El-Majdal road just to the west of the built-up area of 'Iraq Suweidan. Thence it proceeds southward along the western village boundary of El-Faluja to the Beersheba Sub-District boundary. It then runs across the tribal lands of 'Arab El-Jubarat to a point on the boundary between the Sub-Districts of Beersheba and Hebron north of Kh. Khuweilifa, whence it proceeds in a south-westerly direction to a point on the Beersheba-Gaza main road two kilometres to the north-west of the town. It then turns south-eastwards to reach Wadi Sab' at a point situated one kilometer to the west of it. From here it turns north-eastwards and proceeds along Wadi Sab' and along the Beersheba-Hebron road for a distance of one kilometer, whence it turns eastwards and runs in a straight line to Kh. Kuseifa to join the Beersheba-Hebron Sub-District boundary. It then follows the Beersheba-Hebron boundary eastwards to a point north of Ras Ez-Zuweira, only departing from it so as to cut across the base of the indentation between vertical grid lines 150 and 160.

About five kilometres north-east of Ras Ez-Zuweira it turns north, excluding from the Arab State a strip along the coast of the Dead Sea not more than seven kilometres in depth, as far as 'Ein Geddi, whence it turns due east to join the Transjordan frontier in the Dead Sea.

The northern boundary of the Arab section of the coastal plain runs from a point between Minat El-Qila and Nabi Yunis, passing between the built-up areas of Gan Yavne and Barqa to the point of intersection. From here it turns south-westwards, running across the lands of Batani Sharqi, along the eastern boundary of the lands of Beit Daras and across the lands of Julis, leaving the built-up areas of Batani Sharqi and Julis to the westwards, as far as the north-west corner of the lands of Beit-Tima. Thence it runs east of El-Jiya across the village lands of El-Barbara along the eastern boundaries of the villages of Beit Jirja, Deir Suneid and Dimra. From the south-east corner of Dimra the boundary passes across the lands of Beit Hanun, leaving the Jewish lands of Nir-Am to the eastwards. From the south-east corner of Beit Hanun the line runs south-west to a point south of the parallel grid line 100, then turns north-west for two kilometres, turning again in a southwesterly direction and continuing in an almost straight line to the north-west corner of the village lands of Kirbet Ikhza'a. From there it follows the boundary line of this village to its southernmost point. It then runs in a southerly direction along the vertical grid line 90 to its junction with the horizontal grid line 70. It then turns south-eastwards to Kh. El-Ruheiba and then proceeds in a southerly direction to a point known as El-Baha, beyond which it crosses the Beersheba-EI 'Auja main road to the west of Kh. El-Mushrifa. From there it joins Wadi El-Zaiyatin just to the west of El-Subeita. From there it turns to the north-east and then to the south-east following this Wadi and passes to the east of 'Abda to join Wadi Nafkh. It then bulges to the south-west along Wadi Nafkh, Wadi 'Ajrim and Wadi Lassan to the point where Wadi Lassan crosses the Egyptian frontier.

The area of the Arab enclave of Jaffa consists of that part of the town-planning area of Jaffa which lies to the west of the Jewish quarters lying south of Tel-Aviv, to the west of the continuation of Herzl street up to its junction with the Jaffa-Jerusalem road, to the south-west of the section of the Jaffa-Jerusalem road lying south-east of that junction, to the west of Miqve Yisrael lands, to the northwest of Holon local council area, to the north of the line linking up the north-west corner of Holon with the northeast corner of Bat Yam local council area and to the north of Bat Yam local council area. The question of Karton quarter will be decided by the Boundary Commission, bearing in mind among other considerations the desirability of including the smallest possible number of its Arab inhabitants and the largest possible number of its Jewish inhabitants in the Jewish State.

B. THE JEWISH STATE

The north-eastern sector of the Jewish State (Eastern Galilee) is bounded on the north and west by the Lebanese frontier and on the east by the frontiers of Syria and Trans-jordan. It includes the whole of the Huleh Basin, Lake Tiberias, the whole of the Beisan Sub-District, the boundary line being extended to the crest of the Gilboa mountains and the Wadi Malih. From there the Jewish State extends north-west, following the boundary described in respect of the Arab State. The Jewish section of the coastal plain extends from a point between Minat El-Qila and Nabi Yunis in the Gaza Sub-District and includes the towns of Haifa and Tel-Aviv, leaving Jaffa as an enclave of the Arab State. The eastern frontier of the Jewish State follows the boundary described in respect of the Arab State.

The Beersheba area comprises the whole of the Beersheba Sub-District, including the Negeb and the eastern part of the Gaza Sub-District, but excluding the town of Beersheba and those areas described in respect of the Arab State. It includes also a strip of land along the Dead Sea stretching from the

Beersheba-Hebron Sub-District boundary line to 'Ein Geddi, as described in respect of the Arab State.

C. THE CITY OF JERUSALEM

The boundaries of the City of Jerusalem are as defined in the recommendations on the City of Jerusalem. (See Part III, section B, below).

Part III. - City of Jerusalem(5)

A. SPECIAL REGIME

The City of Jerusalem shall be established as a corpus separatum under a special international regime and shall be administered by the United Nations. The Trusteeship Council shall be designated to discharge the responsibilities of the Administering Authority on behalf of the United Nations.

B. BOUNDARIES OF THE CITY

The City of Jerusalem shall include the present municipality of Jerusalem plus the surrounding villages and towns, the most eastern of which shall be Abu Dis; the most southern, Bethlehem; the most western, 'Ein Karim (including also the built-up area of Motsa); and the most northern Shu'fat, as indicated on the attached sketch-map (annex B).

C. STATUTE OF THE CITY

The Trusteeship Council shall, within five months of the approval of the present plan, elaborate and approve a detailed statute of the City which shall contain, inter alia, the substance of the following provisions:

Government machinery; special objectives. The Administering Authority in discharging its administrative obligations shall pursue the following special objectives:

To protect and to preserve the unique spiritual and religious interests located in the city of the three great monotheistic faiths throughout the world, Christian, Jewish and Moslem; to this end to ensure that order and peace, and especially religious peace, reign in Jerusalem;

To foster cooperation among all the inhabitants of the city in their own interests as well as in order to encourage and support the peaceful development of the mutual relations between the two Palestinian peoples throughout the Holy Land; to promote the security, well-being and any constructive measures of development of the residents having regard to the special circumstances and customs of the various peoples and communities.

Governor and Administrative staff. A Governor of the City of Jerusalem shall be appointed by the Trusteeship Council and shall be responsible to it. He shall be selected on the basis of special qualifications and without regard to nationality. He shall not, however, be a citizen of either State in Palestine.

The Governor shall represent the United Nations in the City and shall exercise on their behalf all powers of administration, including the conduct of external affairs. He shall be assisted by an administrative staff classed as international officers in the meaning of Article 100 of the Charter and chosen whenever practicable from the residents of the city and of the rest of Palestine on a non-discriminatory basis. A detailed plan for the organization of the administration of the city shall be submitted by the Governor to the Trusteeship Council and duly approved by it.

3. Local autonomy

The existing local autonomous units in the territory of the city (villages, townships and municipalities) shall enjoy wide powers of local government and administration.

The Governor shall study and submit for the consideration and decision of the Trusteeship Council a plan for the establishment of special town units consisting, respectively, of the Jewish and Arab sections of new Jerusalem. The new town units shall continue to form part the present municipality of Jerusalem.

Security measures

The City of Jerusalem shall be demilitarized; neutrality shall be declared and preserved, and no para-military formations, exercises or activities shall be permitted within its borders.

Should the administration of the City of Jerusalem be seriously obstructed or prevented by the non-cooperation or interference of one or more sections of the population the Governor shall have authority to take such measures as may be necessary to restore the effective functioning of administration.

To assist in the maintenance of internal law and order, especially for the protection of the Holy Places and religious buildings and sites in the city, the Governor shall organize a special police force of adequate strength, the members of which shall be recruited outside of Palestine. The Governor shall be empowered to direct such budgetary provision as may be necessary for the maintenance of this force.

Legislative Organization.

A Legislative Council, elected by adult residents of the city irrespective of nationality on the basis of universal and secret suffrage and proportional representation, shall have powers of legislation and taxation. No legislative measures shall, however, conflict or interfere with the provisions which will be set forth in the Statute of the City, nor shall any law, regulation, or official action prevail over them. The Statute shall grant to the Governor a right of vetoing bills inconsistent with the provisions referred to in the preceding sentence. It shall also empower him to promulgate temporary ordinances in case the Council fails to adopt in time a bill deemed essential to the normal functioning of the administration.

Administration of Justice.

The Statute shall provide for the establishment of an independent judiciary system, including a court of appeal. All the inhabitants of the city shall be subject to it.

Economic Union and Economic Regime.

The City of Jerusalem shall be included in the Economic Union of Palestine and be bound by all stipulations of the undertaking and of any treaties issued therefrom, as well as by the decisions of the Joint Economic Board. The headquarters of the Economic Board shall be established in the territory City. The Statute shall provide for the regulation of economic matters not falling within the regime of the Economic Union, on the basis of equal treatment and non-discrimination for all members of the United Nations and their nationals.

Freedom of Transit and Visit: Control of residents.

Subject to considerations of security, and of economic welfare as determined by the Governor under the directions of the Trusteeship Council, freedom of entry into, and residence within the borders of the City shall be guaranteed for the residents or citizens of the Arab and Jewish States. Immigration into, and residence within, the borders of the city for nationals of other States shall be controlled by the Governor under the directions of the Trusteeship Council.

Relations with Arab and Jewish States. Representatives of the Arab and Jewish States shall be accredited to the Governor of the City and charged with the protection of the interests of their States and nationals in connection with the international administration of the City.

Official languages.

Arabic and Hebrew shall be the official languages of the city. This will not preclude the adoption of one or more additional working languages, as may be required.

Citizenship.

All the residents shall become ipso facto citizens of the City of Jerusalem unless they opt for citizenship of the State of which they have been citizens or, if Arabs or Jews, have filed notice of intention to become citizens of the Arab or Jewish State respectively, according to Part 1, section B, paragraph 9, of this Plan.

The Trusteeship Council shall make arrangements for consular protection of the citizens of the City outside its territory.

Freedoms of citizens

Subject only to the requirements of public order and morals, the inhabitants of the City shall be ensured the enjoyment of human rights and fundamental freedoms, including freedom of conscience, religion and worship, language, education, speech and press, assembly and association, and petition.

No discrimination of any kind shall be made between the inhabitants on the grounds of race, religion, language or sex.

All persons within the City shall be entitled to equal protection of the laws.

The family law and personal status of the various persons and communities and their religious interests, including endowments, shall be respected.

Except as may be required for the maintenance of public order and good government, no measure shall be taken to obstruct or interfere with the enterprise of religious or charitable bodies of all faiths or to discriminate against any representative or member of these bodies on the ground of his religion or nationality.

The City shall ensure adequate primary and secondary education for the Arab and Jewish communities respectively, in their own languages and in accordance with their cultural traditions.

The right of each community to maintain its own schools for the education of its own members in its own language, while conforming to such educational requirements of a general nature as the City may impose, shall not be denied or impaired. Foreign educational establishments shall continue their activity on the basis of their existing rights.

No restriction shall be imposed on the free use by any inhabitant of the City of any language in private intercourse, in commerce, in religion, in the Press or in publications of any kind, or at public meetings.

Holy Places Existing rights in respect of Holy Places and religious buildings or sites shall not be denied or impaired.

Free access to the Holy Places and religious buildings or sites and the free exercise of worship shall be secured in conformity with existing rights and subject to the requirements of public order and decorum.

Holy Places and religious buildings or sites shall be preserved. No act shall be permitted which may in any way impair their sacred character. If at any time it appears to the Governor that any particular Holy Place, religious building or site is in need of urgent repair, the Governor may call upon the community or communities concerned to carry out such repair. The Governor may carry it out himself at the expense of the community or communities concerned if no action is taken within a reasonable time.

No taxation shall be levied in respect of any Holy Place, religious building or site which was exempt from taxation on the date of the creation of the City. No change in the incidence of such taxation shall be made which would either discriminate between the owners or occupiers of Holy Places, religious buildings or sites or would place such owners or occupiers in a position less favourable in relation to the general incidence of taxation than existed at the time of the adoption of the Assembly's recommendations.

Special powers of the Governor in respect of the Holy Places, religious buildings and sites in the City and in any part of Palestine.

The protection of the Holy Places, religious buildings and sites located in the City of Jerusalem shall be a special concern of the Governor. With relation to such places, buildings and sites in Palestine outside the city, the Governor shall determine, on the ground of powers granted to him by the Constitution of both States, whether the provisions of the Constitution of the Arab and Jewish States in Palestine dealing therewith and the religious rights appertaining thereto are being properly applied and respected.

The Governor shall also be empowered to make decisions on the basis of existing rights in cases of disputes which may arise between the different religious communities or the rites of a religious community in respect of the Holy Places, religious buildings and sites in any part of Palestine.

In this task he may be assisted by a consultative council of representatives of different denominations acting in an advisory capacity.

D. DURATION OF THE SPECIAL REGIME

The Statute elaborated by the Trusteeship Council the aforementioned principles shall come into force not later than 1 October 1948. It shall remain in force in the first instance for a period of ten years, unless the Trusteeship Council finds it necessary to undertake a re-examination of these provisions at an earlier date. After the expiration of this period the whole scheme shall be subject to examination by the Trusteeship Council in the light of experience acquired with its functioning. The residents the City shall be then free to express by means of a referendum their wishes as to possible modifications of regime of the City.

Part IV. Capitulations

States whose nationals have in the past enjoyed in Palestine the privileges and immunities of foreigners, including the benefits of consular jurisdiction and protection, as formerly enjoyed by capitulation or usage in the Ottoman Empire, are invited to renounce any right pertaining to them to the re-establishment of such privileges and immunities in the proposed Arab and Jewish States and the City of Jerusalem.

Adopted at the 128th plenary meeting:

In favour: 33

Australia, Belgium, Bolivia, Brazil, Byelorussian S.S.R., Canada, Costa Rica, Czechoslovakia, Denmark, Dominican Republic, Ecuador, France, Guatemala, Haiti, Iceland, Liberia, Luxemburg, Netherlands, New Zealand, Nicaragua, Norway, Panama, Paraguay, Peru, Philippines, Poland, Sweden, Ukrainian S.S.R., Union of South Africa, U.S.A., U.S.S.R., Uruguay, Venezuela.

Against: 13

Afghanistan, Cuba, Egypt, Greece, India, Iran, Iraq, Lebanon, Pakistan, Saudi Arabia, Syria, Turkey, Yemen.

Abstained: 10

Argentina, Chile, China, Colombia, El Salvador, Ethiopia, Honduras, Mexico, United Kingdom, Yugoslavia.

---

(1) See Official Records of the General Assembly, Second Session Supplement No. 11,Volumes l-lV.

* At its hundred and twenty-eighth plenary meeting on 29 November 1947 the General Assembly, in accordance with the terms of the above resolution, elected the following members of the United Nations Commission on Palestine: Bolivia, Czechoslovakia, Denmark, Panama, and Philippines.

(2) This resolution was adopted without reference to a Committee.

(3) The following stipulation shall be added to the declaration concerning the Jewish State: "In the Jewish State adequate facilities shall be given to Arabic-speaking citizens for the use of their language, either orally or in writing, in the legislature, before the Courts and in the administration."

(4) In the declaration concerning the Arab State, the words "by an Arab in the Jewish State" should be replaced by the words "by a Jew in the Arab State."

(5) On the question of the internationalization of Jerusalem, see also General Assembly resolutions 185 (S-2) of 26 April 1948; 187 (S-2) of 6 May 1948, 303 (lV) of 9 December 1949, and resolutions of the Trusteeship Council (Section IV).